IRA
MAN

Talking with the Rebels

Douglass McFerran

PRAEGER

Westport, Connecticut
London

Library of Congress Cataloging-in-Publication Data

McFerran, Douglass, 1934–
      IRA man : talking with the rebels / Douglass McFerran.
         p. cm.
      Includes bibliographical references and index.
      ISBN 0–275–95591–5 (alk. paper)
         1. Ulster (Northern Ireland and Ireland)—History, Military.
      2. Political violence—Ulster (Northern Ireland and Ireland)
      3. Revolutionaries—Ulster (Northern Ireland and Ireland)   4. Irish
      Republican Army.   I. Title.
      DA990.U46M139   1997
      941.6—dc21   97–8862

British Library Cataloguing in Publication Data is available.

Library of Congress Catalog Card Number: 97–8862
ISBN: 0–275–95591–5

First published in 1997

Praeger Publishers, 88 Post Road West, Westport, CT 06881
An imprint of Greenwood Publishing Group, Inc.

Printed in the United States of America

∞

The paper used in this book complies with the
Permanent Paper Standard issued by the National
Information Standards Organization (Z39.48–1984).

10 9 8 7 6 5 4 3 2 1

This book is for Adrienne and for Michael, each of whom made it possible even if in quite different ways.

Contents

Photo essay follows Chapter 6.

Introduction

This is a book about what is happening in Ireland, specifically about the guerrilla war of the group labeled IRA—the Irish Republican Army. Today there are only a few hundred active IRA men, less than a battalion in military terms, who command the attention of some thirty thousand soldiers and policemen in the six northern counties—what is called Ulster or Northern Ireland by the British—and countless more security experts and counterterrorist operatives in England, Europe, and even the United States. To the extent the IRA is able to take the war to its enemy, as it has demonstrated repeatedly through the bombings in England, each volunteer has the potential to disrupt the lives of millions. To understand why this situation ever came about, it is necessary to learn as much as possible about the mind-set not just of the IRA man but also of all those who assist him, since a strong level of support within the community is essential to any successful guerrilla operation.

The task I set myself over a year ago was to get as close as I could to the lived reality of those who call themselves "republicans" (supporters of the Irish Republic envisioned in the rebellion of 1916, depicted in the film *Michael Collins* but, in their eyes, not to be realized until the last British soldier has left Irish soil), and thus think of the IRA as their own army and, to some extent, their only true government. Along the way I became something of an IRA man myself, at least to the extent that I no longer just discussed the IRA but now also defended it.

Allow me to explain.

Ireland is a beautiful island, physically cold but humanly warm. It is also an island with a long history of division determined not by its geography but by decisions made on its neighbor island to the east. Twenty-six of its counties and five-sixths of its landmass, with about three and a half million people, are governed by the Republic of Ireland with its capital in Dublin. The remaining six counties in the northeast of the island, with about a million and a half more people, are part of the United Kingdom and are governed from London. For as long as all but the most elderly Irish can remember, there has been conflict between those who want to end this partition (termed nationalists or republicans) and those who do not (termed unionists or loyalists). This conflict finds its sharpest expression in a guerrilla war waged against the British government by a group that has also been at odds with the government in Dublin since the 1922 adoption of a treaty that established partition. It is a war that most Americans do not understand, and it seems true enough that most British citizens are not any better able to explain it.

I became interested in the current situation when my son, a college student in San Francisco, found himself recruited to help in demonstrations organized by Irish activists. In some ways it seemed he was following in his father's footsteps, since I had been a radical college professor during the turbulent 1960s and had done my share of demonstrating against Washington's policies. What seemed different, though, was that behind the placards and the slogans there was the specter of a group that did not take to the streets in protest marches but instead engaged in systematic assaults on both the police and the military, and through an intensive campaign of bombing had leveled a considerable amount of real estate both in England proper and in the area still referred to as "the province." There was a long history of armed robbery, of kidnapping, and of murder. What, I wondered, could possibly explain all of this? Even if it could be explained, what could ever excuse it?

The impetus for this book came from a young man I will call Kevin Doherty. He was a student, one of the activists my son had met. On one of my visits to San Francisco he posed the possibility of my doing a book about his people and their cause. Almost jokingly, I agreed, on condition I had access to the people who could answer my questions. Phone calls went back and forth between Ireland and San Francisco, and I found that I would be allowed to meet with whomever I wished.

This, then, is a book about what is often called the republican movement, with special attention to its more violent expression through the eighty-year campaign of the group that labels itself in Irish as *Oglaigh na hEireann* (literally, the Irish Volunteers), and in English as the Irish Republican Army—the IRA. To be a republican means to support the cause of a united Ireland free of British control, and insofar as there is a distinction between just being a nationalist and being a "true" republican, it consists in denying the legitimacy of any government that is not the product of a free election throughout all thirty-two counties. The parallel terms on the opposing side are unionist and loyalist, with the distinction tending to be based on how agreeable someone is to allowing any type of Catholic participation in the political life of the north.

I began my research during the euphoria of the cease-fire announced by the Irish Republican Army at the beginning of September 1994. I continued it as the cease-fire broke down and world headlines again declared the casualties from IRA actions. I read as much as I could, talked extensively with Irish activists now residing in the United States, and spent time in both the north and south of Ireland as well as in England. The task I set myself was to understand the truth of the Irish situation, then present this truth in such a way that readers, especially those in the United States, would be better able to grasp it.

I had immense help from supporters of the republican cause both in the United States and in the northern counties. From my choice of titles—speaking of the northern counties rather than of Ulster or "the province," for instance—it will be clear enough that I have been sympathetic to republican goals even if I have been disturbed by the means chosen to achieve them. As a philosopher, even more as a man who once trained for the priesthood, I have never been comfortable with violence, yet I have been asking myself constantly whether there were reasonable alternatives. After all, the United States was born in a bloody revolution and maintained its identity in a bloody civil war—both far more deadly than the events in Ireland—and as an American citizen, I honor the memories of Washington and Lincoln.

There was a French existentialist philosopher, one of the men who lived through the Nazi occupation, who commented that in human events no one can have clean hands. In the Irish situation in particular, moral purity seems to be an unattainable goal, since to act can cause death and not to act can allow death. How things got to be that way will be part of the story I tell. How things might ever be different is what I hope to explain.

There are many ways I could have presented the information in this book. A Catholic bishop, Mark J. Hurley from the California city of Santa Rosa, almost completely avoided lapsing into the first person in his own report, *Blood on the Shamrock*, even when he wrote about a British trooper putting a gun to his head. I am far more partial to the style adopted by the prolific Irish journalist Tim Pat Coogan, who cheerfully introduces the most recent edition of his book *The IRA: A History* by telling the story of how he was in Belfast drinking at a party that included some young IRA men while, unknown to them all until the next morning, eavesdropping British troopers crouched outside the window.

As I insist to my philosophy students, facts never speak for themselves any more than a text can interpret itself. Meaning emerges from an effort to connect things one way rather than another, and it is part of our human experience that we make these connections against the total backdrop of our lives. I hope to justify personal references in the coming chapters—especially my reactions to the places I go and the people I meet—by pointing out that my own life is as much an analytical tool as the formal training I have received in both philosophical analysis and sociological investigation.

For the sake of those with scholarly interests I should be more explicit about my methodology—that sometimes dull stuff about how a writer, especially an academic writer, does his research. My own training in both philosophy and sociology favored a phenomenological approach, which involves getting at meaning from "inside" consciousness rather than from the standpoint of a neutral and presumably dispassionate observer.

What this means is that people and events cannot be studied in the same way as purely physical objects. The goal is not a set of statistical tables allowing limited inferences about causal links but what Max Weber labeled *verstehen*—understanding. The trick is how to get "inside" someone else, and often this is done just by listening to that person talk. Yet to be in the listener's position, I found that I would also have to be the participant-observer, someone who was accepted as willing to act for the cause rather than simply talk about it.

Early on, I understood that many of those I spoke with would not be likely to expose themselves as present or former volunteers, and even others who expressed sympathy for the cause might be reluctant to have their identities exposed, especially if they were legal residents of the United States who, depending on the outlook of the State Department, could face deportation for their support of an illegal "terrorist" organization. Also, I had no intention of wandering on my own through the "bandit country" of areas on the border between north and south just to make contact with active paramilitary units.

Accordingly, I fell back on the device of announcing myself as the American professor who wanted to present the republican view to an audience that was more likely to have seen the IRA demonized in films such as *The Crying Game* and *Patriot Games*. I explained that, with the exception of someone with an international reputation (Gerry Adams, for instance), I would create pseudonyms and as often as not blend some individuals together into a composite character. This proved acceptable, so one person would then talk to me and in turn recommend me to someone else, as well as suggest new lines of inquiry. What I listened for was convergence—the manner in which different individuals would express a common understanding. What I wanted to discover was the basis for the lack of convergence between the republican perspective and its portrayal in the media.

As it turned out, I did not meet with Adams or with Martin McGuinness, the next-best-known figure in Sinn Fein, but as time went on, I found that the truth of the republican situation is that all decisions are ultimately group decisions. Adams did not explain Sinn Fein; it was Sinn Fein—not just this one organization but the concept of a united, independent country proposed early in this century—that explained Adams.

I also did talk, even if in a far more limited manner, with those who see Sinn Fein as their mortal enemy—to the Orangemen, whose annual marches typically spark violent confrontation, and to the Royal Ulster Constabulary (RUC), taunted by republicans as simply another paramilitary force existing to maintain Protestant dominion. As one Sinn Fein official put it, it was a good idea that I did hear the opposite side speak for itself.

To provide a convenient focus, I have presented the setting for all my American interviews as various places in the San Francisco area, but I would insist that no specific place or person be identified just on this basis. Also, I made no tapes and systematically destroyed notes to reduce the possibility that anything in this book could later be used against those who helped me prepare it. If this in any way damages my academic credibility, I accept it as less of an evil than risking a situation in which I might be expected to testify against my informants, all of whom I assured that I would in no way cooperate with any governmental agency here or abroad that might choose to investigate their actions. To that extent I, too, became an auxiliary.

I started my interviews in California and continued them in Ireland itself. "Interview" is probably not the right word. I got into conversations, each time using things I had already been told to generate new questions. At the same time I was reading whatever I could find by other writers who had been over the same intellectual terrain. In presenting all this in the chapters that come, I have gone back and forth between a diary of sorts and a historical analysis that is meant to give the reader otherwise unfamiliar with Irish events some idea of the past that is shaping the present. Finally, I try to make sense of what I have learned.

The result is a book in four parts. The first, in which I also give a very brief review of the historical background, represents the first months of my research and my initial interviews. The second is a more detailed discussion of the past in an effort to establish the forces continuing to affect present perceptions. The third deals with my return to Ireland and a more intensive set of interviews during a critical period in which many expected there to be full-scale civil war. The fourth is an effort to provide a deeper analysis of the issues, with a particular focus on the factors affecting the legitimation of violence.

At the time of writing (spring 1997) there is a continuing standoff in Northern Ireland. Because the IRA ended its cease-fire with "spectaculars" in London and Manchester, Sinn Fein is not allowed to participate in the discussions that are meant to determine the future of the area. The IRA seems unwilling to resume a cease-fire because there was so little progress in serious negotiation from the last one, and now has resumed limited operations in the north. Protestant paramilitaries have carried out sectarian killings but otherwise claim not to be breaking the cease-fire. The talks stumble ahead.

Abbreviations

DUP   Democratic Unionist Party

INLA   Irish National Liberation Army

IRA   Irish Republican Army

IRB   Irish Republican Brotherhood

RUC   Royal Ulster Constabulary

SAS   Special Air Service

SDLP   Socialist Democratic Labor Party

UDA   Ulster Defense Association

UUP   Ulster Unionist Party

UVF   Ulster Volunteer Force

Part I

Republicans Keeping the Faith

One morning early I met armoured cars
Seamus Heaney, "The Toome Road"

1

The Divided Island

The moment the very name of Ireland is mentioned, the English seem to bid adieu to common feeling, common prudence, and common sense, and to act with the barbarity of tyrants, and the fatuity of idiots.

Sydney Smith (1807)

IRELAND: HOW THINGS GOT THE WAY THEY ARE

I first ran across the quotation from Smith in J. Bowyer Bell's 1993 book, *The Irish Troubles*. It is cited frequently in Ireland, and it names as well as anything the central problem in Irish history. For the English, who never questioned their subjugation of other Gaelic-speaking peoples in Wales and Scotland, the addition of Ireland to the British kingdom was simply a matter of manifest destiny. That the Irish saw things differently, and with the sea around them had some hope of their own freedom, was to be a continuing source of frustration. Eighty years ago, following insurrection in the streets of Dublin, the British government attempted to use its army to suppress the Irish rebellion and finally conceded five-sixths of the island. Almost thirty years ago a revitalized IRA began the current war to take back the last one-sixth, which is roughly the size of the island of Hawaii, with lakes instead of mountains in its interior.

For a few pages I am going to expand on this capsule summary, then in later chapters I intend to develop more fully some of the individual points—specifically, British policy in Ireland, the war that ended with the establishment of the modern Irish republic, and the emergence of the current IRA.

The remote history of Ireland—the arrival of a Gaelic-speaking people in perhaps the fourth century BCE, possibly from Spain—is the stuff of legend in which the *Tuatha de Danann* (Danu's people) subjugated still earlier inhabitants and then were displaced by the sons of Mil. Culture heroes such as Cuchulainn, who defended Ulster against the united kings of the rest of Ireland, reflect early divisions that are still part of the mythic structure of the north, even though it is the transplanted Scots who today claim him as their own. What ethnic groups were actually involved is speculative, but the one thing we can be sure of is that, just as virtually everywhere else, no one holds claim to any part of Ireland who did not first assault those who were there earlier. The issue, again as in many other parts of the world, is the extent to which survivors of the assault are willing to press a claim to prior ownership.

The Romans did not make it to Ireland, and, contrary to popular images, neither did the Druids, the Celtic priests who fought against the Romans. The Ireland of the later Roman period was a land of warlords who practiced slavery and did not accept Christianity until a former slave, the man we revere today as Saint Patrick, returned to convert them. That was in the fifth century, but in a few hundred years more the Vikings will begin the raids that eventually exterminated the monastic culture that was Patrick's heritage.

Those Vikings who had settled in France to become the Normans moved beyond England after the Battle of Hastings to extend control over southern Ireland in the days of the twelfth-century mercenary known as Strongbow, whose dark tomb is one of the most interesting features of Christ Church Cathedral in Dublin. The island remained a battleground throughout the Middle Ages as various groups, including the Scots under Robert Bruce, fought for supremacy. By the fourteenth century, England, caught up in internal struggles for power, had ceased to control Ireland, and restoring that control became a key concern of the monarchs from Richard III to the first Elizabeth.

Under Elizabeth's father, the much-married Henry VIII, a fateful new dimension was added to the conflict as England declared its independence from the Church of Rome. The switch from Catholic to Anglican ways, interestingly enough, was not especially problematic for the worldly clergy of Ireland, and the idea that Ireland was fighting to stay Catholic did not really emerge until the time of the Armada, when Irish nobles began to think of the opportunities that might come their way by linking themselves with the Spanish cause. During Cromwell's regime English oppression intensified, and after the Restoration, Irish Catholics made the mistake of siding with James II and his French allies against the Scottish Protestants who had been settled in Ulster early in the century. In Derry the Protestants held out against a deadly siege until they were rescued by William of Orange—the "King Billy" honored with booming lambeg drums in the annual Orangemen parades that too often become the basis for organized violence against Catholic communities.

In the eighteenth century the north, particularly the Belfast area, began playing a more prominent role in British commerce. After the American Revolution broke out, however, Belfast citizens recognized their vulnerability when John Paul Jones attacked and captured a British ship in their waters. Since the government outpost in Dublin was unable to guarantee protection, a Belfast company of scarlet-clad volunteers had already been established on St. Patrick's Day 1778, and with the successful American foray and the entry of France on the American side, other volunteer companies sprang up throughout the Ulster area. These were Protestant units, but part of the intriguing story of the Belfast area is how quickly the volunteers came to see themselves as on the side of Irish independence from England. By 1792, when the mood of the French Revolution was inspiring new calls for independence throughout Europe and the Americas, the volunteers were active in reviving Gaelic culture and in demanding greater political rights for the Catholic minority.

In 1792 the Dublin lawyer Theobald Wolfe Tone, a Protestant who was instrumental in founding the Society of United Irishmen with a charter that called for putting aside religious distinctions, was invited north to assist in spreading the movement. British authorities in Dublin quickly saw its insurrectionist potential and attempted to suppress it in 1797. A year later there was open warfare in County Wexford, to the south of Dublin, between farmers armed with pikes and British regulars armed with muskets and cannon. Wolfe Tone, captured by the British, committed suicide.

From that point on, middle-class Protestants in the north, who had the most to lose when the independence movement foundered and left them open to retribution, identified with the British position. This meant that no longer would idealistic Protestants, specifically the Presbyterians, who themselves were outside the Anglican establishment, stand ready to support the cause of disenfranchised Catholics. In Belfast, Protestants and Catholics—Orangemen and

Ribbonmen a century ago and loyalists and republicans today—
seemed doomed to engage in sectarian conflict.

The Great Famine began in 1845 when a fungus destroyed the
potato crop that was the chief means of subsistence for poorer Irish
families, especially in the southwestern counties. The population of
Ireland dropped sharply through both starvation and massive emigration, and again what was perceived as a failure of the British government led to new calls for independence. In 1858 James Stephens,
who had taken part in an uprising ten years before, established what
was officially called the Irish Republican Brotherhood (the IRB), otherwise known as the Fenians—a reference to the legendary Fiana,
the groups of young warriors remembered in the Ossianic Cycle of
Irish poetry. Under Stephens's direction the Fenian Brotherhood was
organized among Irishmen who saw themselves in exile in New York.
Tough Irish soldiers fought on the Union side in the Civil War, and
many of the veterans then returned to Ireland to help train and lead
their countrymen. On March 4, 1867, the Fenians declared the establishment of the Irish Republic, but the opposition of the Catholic
hierarchy and the efficiency of the police ended the rebellion in just
a few days.

In 1905 the journalist Arthur Griffith set up a group he called Sinn
Fein (pronounced *shin fane* and meaning "ourselves," but with the
sense of "ourselves alone") to promote the idea of a dual monarchy
along the lines of what been settled for Austria and Hungary. Two
years later it melded with the Dungannon Club, organized in Belfast—also in 1905—to revitalize the IRB. The idea of home rule, the
goal of Irish nationalists, did shuffle through Parliament, and this
time the mood of open rebellion appeared in the Protestant rather
than the Catholic community. The Ulster Volunteer Force (UVF) was
organized in 1913 to keep the north free of Catholic control from
Dublin (the fear being that home rule meant "Rome Rule"), and
shortly afterward Irish Catholics in response organized first the Irish
Citizen Army and then the Irish Volunteers.

Civil war was imminent in 1914, but Germany's invasion of Bel-
gium at the outset of the First World War completely changed the
situation. The Irish Volunteers and the Ulster Volunteer Force put
aside their differences to defend the Crown against the Kaiser. The
UVF was allowed to remain as a single unit, which became the 36th
Division, but the nationalists were dispersed among different British
units. Two years later this proved to be a tragic decision when the
36th Division was virtually annihilated in a single attack on the Ger-

man lines, an event recalled in Frank McGuinness's recent play *Observe the Sons of Ulster Marching Towards the Somme.*

Part of the irony of the Easter uprising in 1916 is that while some nationalists were fighting for Britain on the Continent, others had planned a rebellion that would be supported by weapons brought in from Germany. The arms shipment was intercepted, but the leaders went ahead regardless, capturing the post office building in Dublin and issuing still another declaration of an Irish Republic. They were quickly captured, tried, and executed—this last perhaps the worst decision the British government could have made, since it created a set of martyrs and a grand legend that continues to inform the republican spirit. As historian Jonathan Bardon has pointed out, at least twenty thousand Catholic Irishmen had died defending British interests, but it was the few hundred killed in the Easter uprising against those same interests who would be remembered. From this point on, the key force to be reckoned with was the Irish Republican Army that emerged to carry on the struggle.

England attempted to maintain its control in non-Protestant areas during what has come to be called the Tan War as returning Ulster veterans were recruited into an armed auxiliary of British regulars. Eventually a political compromise was reached when the charismatic IRA general Michael Collins agreed to a partition of the island, only to be assassinated for this apparent betrayal of the republican goal. In one of those ironic twists of history, it was Collins's adversary Eamon de Valera who became the first president of what was now called the Free State. Under his rule far more IRA men were imprisoned and executed than in the Easter uprising.

The IRA, outlawed in the south, continued its campaigns, even taking the war to England through a bombing in Coventry in 1939. During the Second World War some IRA men, like their predecessors in 1916, attempted to gain German support, but nothing came of it. The Free State maintained its neutrality—a fact that would long rankle the Belfast Protestants, who saw their city cruelly bombed by Hitler's air force—and IRA efforts sputtered along until February 1962, when the Army Council, officially the small group coordinating IRA activity, ordered the rebels to dispose of their weapons and stand down.

It was the civil rights movement of the late 1960s that again provoked the type of violence that allowed the IRA a new justification for its existence. In particular, the British attack on demonstrators in Derry early in 1972 led to the face-off between Catholic residents in the ghettos of Derry and Belfast that provided the base for a new group, styling itself the Provisional IRA (the Provos), to gain widespread support. Both Martin McGuinness in Derry and Gerry Adams in Belfast were teenagers who quickly moved forward to prominence in their communities, eventually relinquishing the anonymity of IRA fighters for the public attention of Sinn Fein spokesmen. What came to be called the Long War had begun, but the IRA had also taken on a new political sophistication.

On August 31, 1994, the IRA announced a cease-fire. Loyalist militias acceded to it, and for nearly a year and a half the north would experience a lack of violence and intimidation that for the teenagers living there was unprecedented. British proposals for how to proceed diplomatically soon came to be seen as stalling tactics, however, and on February 9, 1996, Sinn Fein president Gerry Adams, who seemed genuinely surprised by the decision, called the White House to announce that the IRA had ended the cease-fire. An hour later a massive bomb went off in one of the key financial areas of London, and in accepting responsibility the IRA served notice that their guerrilla war would continue. On February 18 Edward O'Brien, a young Irishman living almost invisibly in London, became the first volunteer to die in the new campaign when a bomb he was transporting went off prematurely.

DUBLIN: JUNE 1995

We arrived in Dublin the same spring day as did Prince Charles, though far less regally, with suitcases that we hefted on and off a bus from the airport and again up the steps to our bed and breakfast. My wife of thirteen years had finally convinced me to venture away from North America, and it was her conviction that I should at least see the land of my ancestors. I had been less sure. The Ireland I tended to identify with was not the divided land of the present but, because of the research I had done for other books, the more ancient world of pagan bards yet to hear Saint Patrick's preaching. Modern Ireland was the land from which my family had escaped some generations back, and I had a racial memory of it as a somber country of famine and futility in which a man's death might be justly celebrated with a drunken wake, and his life recalled as a struggle against the elements and the callous rule of distant English lords. Also, as a lapsed Catholic, I was not altogether comfortable coming to a place where the currency featured the wimpled face of a saintly nun. Would there be shrines to the Blessed Virgin at the airport, I wondered—and would everyone stop to pray the Angelus at noontime?

It was late afternoon, and although we had already been awake more than twenty-four hours, we decided to walk along the Liffey a few blocks to downtown Dublin and O'Connell Street. Already I was experiencing an odd sense of homecoming. My wife commented that with my gray beard and ruddy face and snub nose, I looked just like any other old guy on the street, and I thought I saw my daughter's twin in every redheaded girl walking by. Indeed, this was a place with a quite limited gene pool. Maybe my wife was right: all us Irish looked alike—and I thought we looked pretty good.

I had not known Prince Charles was in Dublin that evening, but I soon learned of it as I was handed a flyer announcing a protest march starting at the bridge. Various groups were assembling to walk the streets to Dublin Castle, where the British heir to the throne was dining in state. For my wife and myself it was like being transported back to the 1960s. The Irish *gardai*, black-clad policemen, were out in force, and for a while I had visions of Chicago during the Democratic convention of 1968.

Cautiously we moved into the rear of the march itself. It seemed safe enough, especially if we stayed close to the women with baby strollers. It took a long while before the people with the banners were ready to start off, but eventually we were under way. We soon saw that the *gardai* were there to escort us along, obviously careful that we kept to the appointed route but otherwise not in the least intimidating. And so my wife and I marched and joined in the raucous chants, one of which rhymed "queen" and "guillotine" while others drummed "para, para, para," a reference to the fact that Charles was the titular commander of the paratroop unit that had opened fire on unarmed protestors on a Sunday afternoon in Derry in January 1972. As I was to read later, many of the fifteen hundred marchers were from Derry and Belfast and the other areas caught up in the escalating violence that had followed "Bloody Sunday."

After a few blocks a young man with a microphone leaped in front of us. We were live on an Irish radio station, and he wanted to know why we were marching. I had been thinking all along of my son, a college student in San Francisco who had been recovering his roots through intensifying involvement in Irish activism. I knew he had taken part in demonstrations in the Bay Area, and, as I said to the reporter, I felt that this was what he would have been doing had he the chance to be here in Dublin. That was not enough for the young man. Why march at all, he asked. I said the obvious thing: I was joining all these others to protest the centuries of British oppression.

What I almost said was that even though I was from the United States, this was my country and I wanted the British out of it.

My country? In just a few hours I had blown away the cobwebs in my thinking—the reluctance to "wear the green" and celebrate my ethnicity on Saint Patrick's Day, the discomfort with acknowledging the Catholic upbringing that had taken me to the life of a Jesuit seminarian, the cautious impartiality with which I had talked about the Troubles as though both sides, the Protestant and the Catholic, were equally to blame. For the moment, at least, I was Irish and Catholic and entirely on the side of those who had taken up the gun when no other means were left.

Further down I found a phone booth, and after fumbling around to figure out the mystery of an access code, I used my phone card to call my son at his apartment in San Francisco. I held up the phone for him to hear the drums and the chanting, and I told him to tell his Irish friends that I was thinking of them.

That is possibly what started off this book. Michael had already told the people he knew that I was a college professor and an author with several titles, both fiction and nonfiction, to his credit. Also, I had asked his friend Kevin Doherty, who would turn out to be one of the central figures in organizing the interviews that appear in this book, to check up on what had happened to a former Irish prisoner who had once had his letter to another author misdirected to me by my London publisher. Kevin in turn had asked Michael about my interest in doing a book dealing with Sinn Fein, the Irish party typically identified as the political wing of the Irish Republican Army. Now I found myself much more interested in the possibility.

Kevin was concerned with my choice for a title (*IRA Man*). So often there is an effort to distance the Irish cause from association with an illegal paramilitary organization that there is a pretense that Gerry Adams and Martin McGuinness, now the most prominent individuals in Sinn Fein, have never been warriors but only politicians. My own thinking was that I needed to tell the story of the IRA, and since Adams and McGuinness have been the key figures in the peace talks that have held the headlines since September 1994, it was hardly reasonable to treat Sinn Fein as an entirely distinct organization. Eventually I proposed a few alternatives and asked the activists themselves to sort them out.

But this all was later. In the chill and blustery days of early June, tramping through the streets of Dublin on the wonderful walking tours recommended to the hardy tourist, I was still attempting to understand this country. Possibly the most striking thing was that Dublin seemed so little Catholic by comparison with other cities I had visited, even in my own United States. Catholic kitsch—Marian shrines and ornate pictures of the Sacred Heart—definitely were not part of the decor of Dublin Airport. Far more important, the great institutions—Christ Church Cathedral and Trinity College, for instance—were still clearly Protestant. Most of the great buildings we toured were relics of British rule, and in the artwork there were considerable reminders of the fact that from Henry VIII to Elizabeth II, British monarchs have claimed to be the head of the Church of England.

I came to appreciate something more about the Irish-American experience—the importance of a grand edifice such as New York's Saint Patrick's Cathedral and the symbolism of the Saint Patrick's Day marches in which even the most unlikely individuals for a day display themselves as Irishmen. My mother, who was from New York, had told me of what it was like for her as a young girl, growing up when Irish males were stereotyped as drunken, illiterate brawlers and Irish females were sterotyped as capable of only the most menial jobs. Even in Los Angeles, to which she had come in the heyday of the Ku Klux Klan, she had been asked her religion and told that no Catholics would be hired by the large firm where she had gone to apply for a job. Growing up in a parish staffed by Irish-born priests, I had been taught to beware association with Protestants in the same way as young Jews—my wife, for instance—were so often taught to beware association with Gentiles. It was not hatred as such, but simply a profound distrust of the outsider who was believed to hate us for our religion. For us Irish, as for those who were Jewish, it did not matter so much that you were an example of the faith. What counted was that when the chips were down, you did not identify with the enemy.

In the United States the Irish infiltrated the establishment just as the Jews did, but having a slightly earlier start, their success was greater. The Irish became the cops and then the politicians, and eventually with John F. Kennedy they showed that the last barriers had been broken through. By the 1960s being Irish or even being Catholic was no longer particularly important, as I learned when I was invited to lecture at a Catholic girls' high school and found the sisters teaching there attempting to have their charges see themselves simply as Christians, without any special emphasis on denominational differences.

In the Republic of Ireland only one person in twenty is not nominally Catholic, and paradoxically this may explain why there is so little evidence of a specifically Catholic identity. Unlike the United States a few generations back, there is not much need for Catholics to prove anything to those around. A staple of contemporary Irish fiction is the Catholic youngster who blithely ignores the moral strictures of the Church. A sad reality is the extent to which the Irish clergy, beset with scandals that range from a prelate's offspring to multiple examples of pedophile priests, appear to ignore them as well.

The anthropologist Mary Douglas has documented the manner in which, in the days before Catholic rules were changed, Irish workingmen in London took the demand not to eat meat on Friday as a way of establishing their distinctive identity. In the wake of Vatican II a survey indicated that abolishing this rule was among the most upsetting things to American Catholics because they became less sure of how they did differ from Protestants. Again, it seems, there is a question of having something visible to establish a separateness so long as it seems important to remain separate.

In Dublin, I realized, there were things that marked a strong religious influence—instances were the shuttered stores on Sunday and the debate on whether to legitimize divorce for couples who had already been living apart—but this was also a city that had had a Jewish mayor and continued to have strong Protestant links.

There was the joke some years back, at the height of the Troubles, about the tourist confronted by a man with a knife who asks him his religion. Afraid that his attacker is a Catholic, he will not say he is a Protestant, and yet if he says he is a Catholic, he might be slain by an angry Protestant. His solution is to call out that he is Jewish, upon which the other man announces that he is the luckiest Arab in all Ireland. I knew now that this story could never have been set in Dublin. I was never asked my religion, and even though there is a possibility that an American tourist could be exempted from religious scrutiny as already among the hell-bent, I really did not have the feeling that my beliefs, or lack thereof, much mattered. Religious intensity, in a safely monolithic society, fails to have much political significance. It really does become a private matter: some are saints but most are sinners, and the system is not much challenged by either.

The day after the march there were many thousands of Dubliners along O'Connell Street. This time they had come to watch Prince Charles officially open the new office of the British Trade Authority. Obviously welcomed by the crowd, Charles took a walk down the street toward Trinity College. Someone was arrested for throwing an egg, and I did hear a few faint shouts, but the protesters of the night before were not otherwise visible at all. Just when I was getting used to thinking of Charles in a more politically correct manner as plain Mr. Windsor, I found the Irish quite delighted to have one of the royals among them for the first time since independence. Their one regret seemed to be that he had already separated from Princess Diana, so they could not see her as well.

That afternoon, as Kevin had suggested I should, I found my way to a Sinn Fein bookstore. It was a small place in one of the Georgian apartment buildings with the brightly painted doors that are so distinctive of Dublin, and it reminded me of so many of the little holes in the wall of the 1960s in which scrawny teenagers sold revolutionary tracts. There were just a few books for sale along with some buttons and bumper stickers. I bought a couple of bumper stickers from a bored youngster. Maybe I could have engaged him in an intense political discussion, but somehow I doubted that I would find any level of sophistication.

Where, I asked myself, were all the young rebels, those who were the recruits ready to do and die for the IRA? They were certainly not here in Dublin, which seemed little concerned about the six northern counties remaining in the United Kingdom. I found one piece of graffiti—"Up the Provos"—but little indication otherwise that Sinn Fein or the IRA really had that much significance. Once in the street I did see a few young people selling banners that I thought commemorated one or another group of prisoners; inquiring about the name, I found that they were advertising a new rock band appearing in the city.

Attempting to find parallels with what I knew from the United States, I thought of attitudes in northern cities during the initial civil rights activities in the south. In Chicago or New York, where blacks were not being lynched, places like Birmingham seemed to be in a completely different world where change might come only at a snail's pace and could not be hurried by misguided outsiders. It was better not to get involved.

In the twenty-six counties comprising the Irish Republic, there seemed to be the same indifference. Just be glad you're not a Catholic in the north—just like you should be glad you're not a black in the American south. Agitation is not the answer, especially since it risks bringing the violence below the border. In fact, there might not be any answer, but then you don't live there yourself—and you will make every effort to limit the disturbances caused by those who do. What surprise was there, then, that the only evidence I had of Sinn Fein was a few scruffy youngsters—and why should I be astonished that Charles was given a genuinely royal welcome?

I left Ireland with a number of questions. The most serious was whether the Irish government itself could have any real interest in reunification if it meant having to deal with a distinctive Protestant minority angered by a reversal of fortune. The express aim of the IRA had been not just an end to British military presence but the complete severance of links with the United Kingdom. My bumper sticker read "26 + 6 = Ireland." But what if the twenty-six counties to the south were quite content not to have to deal with the problems of the six counties to the north?

I realized I understood altogether too little. I had only the most sketchy picture of the history of Irish independence, and later in London, where my wife and I attended a performance of Sean O'Casey's classic *The Plough and the Stars*, about the doomed Easter Rebellion, I had to ask whether even now there was a coherent political program that would lead the north beyond its tortured present.

I knew I had a lot to ask the rebels, even though it had not yet occurred to me that the rebels were open to being asked. Months later, with a contract in hand and the continued assurance of full cooperation, I had to work through a procedure for my interviews. What I decided on was a completely conversational approach, in the hope that enough would emerge for me to put together a coherent picture of the IRA and its supporters. Above all, I wanted to verify something Kevin kept insisting on: these were not hardened gunmen but deeply moral individuals who felt justified in using extralegal and sometimes lethal means to achieve their vision of Irish freedom.

Security would be an issue, I realized. Some of those I spoke with might be wanted men, and others would be concerned that what they said could be used against relatives and friends. Also, some of the things I would most like to know about were not past actions but plans for the future, and clearly no one in any position of authority could risk jeopardizing either a diplomatic or a military action by speaking too freely. I decided early on to make it clear to my informants that I should not be told anything that it would be inappropriate for me to know—and this would be as much for my protection as for theirs.

At the beginning I knew I wanted to do at least this much: establish the extent to which generally unsympathetic portrayals of the IRA in films such as *Patriot Games, The Crying Game,* and *Blown Away* (with Tommy Lee Jones speaking Irish) had a basis in fact. Were there moral limits to the actions undertaken—or was it the case that the end would always justify the means?

I had a deeply personal reason for wanting to know this. My son as a teenager had survived the risks of being caught up in a gang, even though the tiny group he was with was hardly anything like the Crips and Bloods who ruled the streets of the inner city in Los Angeles. He had been in enough fights, certainly, and the fact that none of them involved gunfire was probably more a matter of luck than of conscience. I could understand his identification with a young Irishman who becomes the volunteer—the actual foot soldier in the IRA's underground legion. Was he linking himself to a lie, I wondered. Did he uncritically accept a conveniently sanitized picture of the Irish rebels, one that made them out to be reluctant killers forced to pull the trigger only as a desperate last resort?

But it was not just my son I was thinking about. What if I were now in Ireland, and there came a time when I had to choose between the law and the dream? Would I stand by the dreamers—or stand against them? Brian Moore, an internationally respected Catholic novelist from Belfast who is so good at depicting struggles of conscience, essentially answered the question one way—against the IRA— in his chilling novel *Lies of Silence*. A more ambiguous position appeared in Edna O'Brien's *House of Splendid Isolation*, in which an aging Irish widow shields a gunman on the run. Even as an American, should I be like the Dubliners, glad it is someone else's problem, or should I seek a more personal involvement?

Even writing this book brings up a moral issue. I was going to make it plain to my Irish contacts that if I found a real problem in presenting Sinn Fein and the IRA sympathetically, I would ask to have my contract rescinded rather than violate the hospitality I would be shown. Under no condition did I intend to deal with the authorities, here or in Britain or in the Republic. Yet what if my book did end up providing support for a group that, as far as I knew, was responsible for a number of horrific killings in the past and might yet be responsible for more in the future?

As an author I had already written about subjects that might be disturbing. My decision, obviously, was to go with the project—and I did not find my conscience bothering me in the least. What I could hope for was that if I did my job well, something of what I saw would help bring an end to the situation that made the IRA a seeming necessity.

2

"We Are All Volunteers"

She remembers being at a funeral and how someone had said that
both lots should be put in a stadium and made to shoot one
another in rotation, a prolonged blitz until they were a heap of
carnage, twined and twisted like the innocents they had killed, and
how a distraught woman had stood up and in a croaking voice said,
"You've forgotten your country's wrongs," whereupon people had
moved away from her, realising that she was a sympathiser.
                        Edna O'Brien, *House of Splendid Isolation*

SAN FRANCISCO: NOVEMBER 1995

I have never needed much of an excuse to return to San Francisco,
where I lived and worked from 1959 to 1962. Living in the city, it was
impossible to escape the Irish influence, but in those years I was still
living down my heritage rather than taking any greater interest in
exploring it. I was a member of the Jesuit order assigned to teach
Spanish at Saint Ignatius High School, just outside of Golden Gate
Park by the campus of the Jesuit-run University of San Francisco.
This period of teaching—regency, we called it—was unique to the
Jesuits, a deliberate interruption in the formal studies for the priesthood that had the advantage of giving the young seminarian (the
proper term was "scholastic") a chance to experience more of what
his life would be after ordination in a group that essentially was
dedicated to education. My experience had the effect of leading me

to reconsider just what I wanted to do with my life, and it was somewhat ironic that I ended up still teaching, first mathematics at a military school in Brentwood, then philosophy at a community college in the San Fernando Valley.

For anyone familiar with San Francisco politics, the role of the Irish in the Democratic party is well known. Less well known is how many of the individuals who are the political and cultural leaders have a strong identification with the Irish republican movement. What I was to realize quickly was that these republicans were by no means a fringe group seduced by extremist fantasies. They were among the city's most respected citizens, and whatever their caution in expressing support for the IRA, they could be counted on to do their part.

By now I had done a little more reading on the recent history of Ireland and was paying special attention to the fortunes of the revived Irish Republican Army, especially the self-styled Provisionals or Provos. Gerry Adams and Martin McGuinness, the lead figures from Sinn Fein in the negotiations that had followed the cease-fire, were said to have held command positions in the Provos in the actions of the 1970s. My son had gone with Kevin to hear Adams speak in San Francisco, and gave me a picture of a man who might easily have been hailed as an Irish Moses leading his people out of bondage yet apparently did not encourage being seen as anything more than a team player in what everyone hoped was the final period of play between British overlords and Irish rebels.

I had to admit that Adams interested me immensely. Without a college education he had still made his mark as an author, highly commended in a review by Jimmy Breslin for the collection of short stories published as *The Street*. As a novelist myself I could fantasize a conversation in which Gerry and I would discuss politics only indirectly. Instead we would explore the depths of the Irish soul and part with a deep bond that might, at some point, entitle me to a privileged call to serve a new Irish government. Fantasy? Well, I might very much enjoy talking with Adams the writer, but I would definitely be worried about Adams the politician if he thought of me as a politician.

A more immediate concern was establishing a working relationship with the expatriate Irish in California. Kevin prepped me on the concern for security. There had already been the experience of someone—a woman presenting herself as an immigration lawyer—coming close to one group in order to tip off the American government on the whereabouts of several of the men who had escaped the Maze—the prison for IRA men in Northern Ireland—in 1983. One of the escapees was Jimmy Smyth, who had become very vocal in his own defense as the government worked for his extradition. My son's more direct involvement with Irish activism had been through helping Kevin Doherty arrange for Jimmy to speak at San Francisco State, much to the horror of the British consulate. At the time I had joked that now he would have an FBI file of his own, set right behind mine.

What seemed to convince the activists to accept me was that I had spent ten years as a scholastic. My having been with the Society of Jesus did have an interesting effect on people, I realized. I had once been told, although not by an especially reliable source, that the CIA decided not to maintain any intensive surveillance on me during my activist days a quarter-century back because as an ex-Jesuit I was unlikely to be *that* subversive. And I could always tell the story of how, over a bottle of beer at a Jesuit vacation villa, I gave Jerry Brown an early lecture on the positions of the existentialists. A year later Jerry left the Jesuits, supposedly for being too "existentialist," and later quoted the existentialist author Camus while running for the office of state governor. With the republicans my Jesuit background probably seemed subversive enough on its own that I would be less likely to turn out to be the tout—the informer.

I drafted a statement that I would give each person I interviewed. It stated who I was and what I was working on, and it also expressed my commitment to accept imprisonment, if need be, rather than cooperate with the authorities by revealing any information that could be useful in a criminal action. As a journalist, I said bravely, I was protected by the "shield law" in place in California, but I knew that elsewhere there might not be any particular privilege for writers. However, by not making tapes or keeping notes I hoped that I was making the point that it would be useless to subpoena me.

It did seem important to the people I first talked with that I not use their names, and they generally agreed to my proposal that I would present their stories and their views through fictionalized composite characters. What I wanted to present, after all, was something I would call the truth of the situation. Also, the questions I chose to ask would develop as my own understanding matured. I hoped that by the time I had worked my way to the top, I would be posing exactly the right questions and the answers I got would allow a fresh perspective on what now was happening in Ireland.

Paul, who was from County Cork in the south, was in his forties. We had agreed to meet as a small group in one of San Francisco's many Irish pubs, and I had my pint of Guinness and he was working on his final whiskey. He seemed eager that I establish my family links. I told him that my family name was a northern one—I had found some servants with this name listed in an 1850 census of County Antrim—but I speculated that my maternal grandfather, Joseph Nagle, had his roots in Cork. What I did know for sure was that his wife, Mary Henry, was a Catholic born in Edinburgh and raised as an orphan in a New York convent.

Since everyone was following the peace talks with the expectation of President Clinton's visit to Ireland later in the month, I wanted some idea of how Paul felt about their chance of success. He answered brusquely. They were a mistake, since the British could never be trusted and must be driven out with bullets.

This was the strongest answer I got, but the general tone of all there was quite pessimistic. No one was giving Gerry Adams much hope of pulling off what until now had been unthinkable—a negotiated withdrawal of British troops leading to new elections in Northern Ireland that eventually would lead to reunification. The British insistence on what was called "decommissioning"—the surrender of all weapons held by paramilitary groups—seemed evidence of bad faith. Paul might talk about driving the Brits out as though this could be done through firepower, but everyone else saw the need of an armed force in more defensive terms. Even if the British did withdraw, this would only put the situation back to where it had been in the early 1970s, when Ulstermen terrorized the minority Catholic population in Belfast and Derry.

I had been hearing for a while now that the cease-fire, in place for a little over a year, would soon break down. Kevin reported the gossip that there was serious dissension within the IRA, with many units chafing at the bit. Already I was being advised that a planned return trip to Ireland should take place before the early spring, when there might again be widespread bombing. It was hardly a pleasant thought, but it inspired another question that I posed to several of my informants. What, I wondered, was the likelihood that individuals as disaffected as Paul would attempt to sabotage the talks by provocative bits of violence?

This was a hard question to answer. Adams and those close to him had been involved in secret negotiations with the British long before the cease-fire, and those linked to the IRA ranks in Ireland had little knowledge of what was happening until they heard the public announcements. Those in America were at an even greater disadvantage because they had to rely on old friends still in Ireland for inside information. Generally, though, everyone was willing to give Adams a chance, but there was still the pervasive feeling that the British government was not to be trusted. Some seemed to favor a start-and-stop approach: negotiate, then suspend the cease-fire if negotiation stalled and resume it when the British got the message, which might not happen until a few bombs had gone off.

I thought back to a few people I had chatted with in Dublin and in London earlier in the year. They were from the north and had this tremendous sense of relief that the Troubles were coming to an end. A start-and-stop approach would, I thought, have a devastating effect from a public relations perspective. It would be the IRA and not the British who were seen at fault, and this could only serve to weaken Adams's position.

I asked about the so-called punishment beatings and shootings that had escalated in intensity in recent months. According to the news reports, IRA squads were involved in a number of actions in Catholic areas that were mostly directed at alleged drug dealers. What puzzled me was the element of torture coming into play in some of the reports. Torture had been a characteristic of Protestant terrorism in past years, and I was curious about whether some of the reported incidents attributed to the IRA might have been staged by their opposition, again as a way of sabotaging the talks.

Martin and Thomas, still closely connected to people in the north, both defended the concept of punishment beatings and shootings. As Martin explained to me, in a Catholic area, such as the Bogside in Derry or Falls Road in Belfast or anywhere else that there was clear sectarian segregation, you did not call on the RUC, the Royal Ulster Constabulary, to deal with criminal activity. The RUC, now almost entirely Protestant in its membership and often siding openly with Protestant mobs in the past, had effectively forfeited its position as the defender of law and order. The Catholics had to police their own, even if this called for summary justice. Despite the tendency of the press to portray the IRA as attempting to "control the rackets," the republican belief was that drug dealers represented too severe a threat to the community to be allowed to operate with impunity. As for my question about provocation, I was told that it was difficult to tell whether in any given incident those involved had really been IRA men since actions of this kind were within the discretion of local IRA leaders, who were under no obligation to come forward to accept responsibility.

One thing neither Martin nor Thomas discussed was whether they had themselves been volunteers—active members of the IRA and not just Sinn Fein activists. Kevin had already cued me that this was essentially something off limits, and the more I was to learn about the IRA, the more I realized the applicability of the old Chinese maxim that he who knew did not speak and he who spoke did not know. Martin did tell me this much: with the tradition of secrecy, no one of the enemy could know who was a volunteer, and to that extent "we are all volunteers." It was one of those enlightening remarks that allowed many other things to come into perspective, and as he said it, I experienced a minor bit of *satori*, as though at last I understood the meaning of one hand clapping.

In my preliminary reading I had run across references to the *Green Book*, a training manual for volunteers developed in the early 1970s. It was here that the idea of secrecy was given special emphasis: a volunteer did not tell his family or his fiancée or anyone else about his connection with the IRA. Asked whether copies of the *Green Book* were ever in the hands of volunteers, Martin laughed and pointed out that a young man might as well be carrying his own death warrant. One time, he said, British soldiers had ransacked his family's house, and they had gone through all the books that were there. Their finding the *Green Book* would have been enough to have everyone in the household detained and interrogated in a manner made familiar to Americans who saw the film *In the Name of the Father* and once defended by English authorities on the basis that it was not torture because the interrogators did not enjoy inflicting pain.

Repeatedly I was hearing references to the everyday situation of Catholics in areas where the British concentrated their efforts. Neither Martin nor Thomas had been detained, but they had been roughed up repeatedly, as though beating up Catholic teens would have the salutary effect of warning them away from violence. Thomas, who was from the more rural area of County Fermanaugh rather than the mean streets of Belfast and Derry, talked about the need of keeping the family dogs inside the house at night. British practice was to kill the dogs that were out, since their barking would alert those around to the presence of a patrol. Beatings, warrantless searches, detention on the basis of a mere suspicion—these were all actions characteristic of an occupying army rather than of a peacekeeping force, as the British military role had initially been defined when Ulster violence and IRA retaliation had escalated in the 1970s.

Kevin, who had already had many conversations with former volunteers, attempted to sum up some of their attitudes before I began the interviews. Imagine, he said, being a teenager who has seen the abuse of his friends and neighbors and is then asked to do something fairly simple, such as keeping a lookout. Gradually, as he shows he can be trusted, he is given more dangerous assignments that finally involve him in the life of a volunteer. This would be only for a few years, since most volunteers were not yet married and did not have the type of responsibility that would have compromised their enthusiasm. Did this also mean, I asked Martin, that a volunteer had to be "blooded"—take part in a shooting—before he was completely trusted? Martin said simply that a volunteer had to be ready to take part in a war and left me to draw my own conclusions.

How Catholic were these men? Martin did not have much use for the Church—the Irish hierarchy had constantly distanced itself from the republican movement—but Thomas attended Mass regularly and in his celibate lifestyle reminded me very much of the type of individual who might have been drawn to the seminary and ended up in an American parish. I asked Thomas whether overt Catholicism played much of a role with those he knew within Sinn Fein. No, he said, he was hardly typical, although Martin McGuinness was known for being very devout. Even though everyone talked about the Catholic cause, more properly the division was between Irish nationalists and those who favored union with Great Britain. Republicans were typically Catholic, but this was not a religious war, much less a Vatican-linked *jihad*. After all, the first great defender of Irish freedom had been Wolfe Tone, who was Protestant, and in the 1930s and 1940s there had been a number of Protestants involved with the IRA in Belfast.

Others I talked with came back to the same theme. Despite the vicious anti-Catholic oratory of Ian Paisley, the issue was not religion but Irish autonomy. Ulstermen desperately wanted to see themselves as British, not Irish, even though a Belfast Protestant in London would be instantly recognizable from his accent and would still be as likely to experience discrimination—be seen as just another "paddy"—as his Catholic neighbor. We could talk about the "Prods," but it was their political and not their religious outlook that we had in mind. The IRA man was most likely just a nominal Catholic himself. Giving a greater role to the Church, which seemed the thing most feared by many unionists in the event of reunification, was hardly what he had in mind.

I thought back to my few days in Dublin months before. Many of those who marched to protest the royal visit would just as likely have marched to protest the Pope, and I remembered the uproar Sinead O'Connor had caused when at a concert she had torn up a picture of John Paul II. The constant emphasis on sectarian conflict that I found in the press was definitely misleading, at least as a representation of the IRA outlook. The unionist focus on religion, particularly on an exaggerated view of Catholicism that made some sense in the last century, when Vatican pronouncements were a force to be reckoned with, but seemed hopelessly outdated in the fractured Church of the present, more a way of evading the real issue of a formerly privileged group adapting to a changing situation. The IRA in its turn was anti-British but not anti-Protestant.

Yet even here there was not so much a hatred of things English—a rampant Anglophobia such as I had seen when visiting Montreal and Quebec—as a demand that Irish autonomy be respected. The revival of the rather difficult Irish language, ironically a result of the work of Protestant antiquarians in the north, had played some role in creating a specific sense of Irish identity, and in Dublin I had been surprised to hear the amount of Irish spoken, particularly by younger people. Still, the fact of the matter was that Irish was something studied in school and given limited exposure otherwise—a page or so in the newspaper and a few spots on the radio band. Most people could not speak it easily and had little interest in doing so. IRA men in prison camps had undertaken the task of teaching it to each other as much to have something to do as to frustrate their British guards. There was certainly no serious effort to replace English with Irish as evidence of revolutionary purity.

Because I was in San Francisco and not yet in Belfast, much of the conversation came back to local causes—to the treatment of Irish prisoners by the American authorities. James was another young American who, like my son, had involved himself in the Irish cause. Through him I learned of the international group Saiorse that tracked those who were being held in British and American custody. I was given a small green ribbon, like the red AIDS ribbon, and told that the Gaelic word *saoirse* (pronounced *seer-shaw*) meant "freedom." James was himself committed to nonviolence, but that had not affected his support for those IRA men now imprisoned. His special concern otherwise was for those imprisoned not because they were volunteers but because they were accused of supporting the IRA in some other manner.

One such person was a young woman whom I will call Jennifer Pearse, like my son a graduate of San Francisco State College, who had worked as an electrical engineer and was charged with conspiracy for using classified information to assist a supposed IRA effort to build more sophisticated weaponry. In discussing her case I told James something more about my own days as a radical college professor connected with allegedly subversive organizations such as the Black

Students' Union and Students for a Democratic Society. He was too young to remember what I did about FBI efforts to protect democracy by infiltrating their own informants, who would often attempt to create an incident—possibly in itself just a misdemeanor—because of which otherwise innocent individuals could be arrested on a felony charge of conspiracy. Jennifer had paid a heavy price for her involvement with Irish activists: a sentence of three and a half years in prison. I made a note to see what could be done about interviewing her.

With Kim, who for the most part sat by quietly while I talked with Paul and Martin and Thomas and James, I found other questions. I always heard of the IRA men, seldom of IRA women, even though there had been some very prominent female figures, such as the murdered Maire Drumm. What was a woman's place in the new Irish vision? Stubbing out one cigarette and lighting another, she asked me sardonically if I had all night. The Irish, she said, had yet to come to grips with the issues of gender and class, but these would be the real problems down the road.

A list of Irish prisoners went on for pages, and I was told that there were more than five hundred men and women incarcerated in the United States, England, or the north of Ireland. Many of these prisoners had families who depended on financial assistance from groups such as Noraid (Irish Northern Aid), to which Kevin had belonged for several years.

One thing that struck me in these initial conversations was how few people seemed to be that actively involved. I asked whether there had ever been more of an effort to create a mass movement along the lines of what we had had during the Vietnam period. I was told that actually this had been somewhat discouraged. What matters, Thomas explained, is that there is a small group, probably no more than six or eight individuals, who could work in harmony. Forced to choose between relative obscurity and some kind of mass movement, Thomas favored obscurity because it allowed a greater degree of control.

I realized as he spoke that his outlook was a very special key to understanding how the IRA had managed to persevere despite all the efforts of British authorities to suppress it. An IRA man was not a soldier of fortune, nor was he a naive idealist captivated by romantic illusions. He was simply someone who saw it was his turn to help his friends, even at the risk of his life. He had to be someone known and vouched for, not an outsider who might be an informer or worse. He would get only token pay—no uniform, no special status in his community. Public recognition came if he were captured or killed, but that was not an invitation to solicit martyrdom. If he took advantage of his position, as sometimes happened when a volunteer settled a private score or engaged in criminal acts apart from authorized "acts of war" (which at one point had included robberies), he could be court-martialed and punished, perhaps by having a bullet put through his kneecap, perhaps by being executed.

Persistence was the secret. Martin and Thomas were from the first generation of young Irishmen to know nothing but violence, and even then they saw their efforts as part of a crusade for Irish independence already two centuries old. They were not going to be disillusioned if the present peace talks failed. Both had come to the United States for the simple reason that they lacked opportunities for economic success in their own country, but they had not been ready to abandon those who remained. The Irish cause was not going to dry up and blow away.

I still had my original questions about the chances Sinn Fein had for achieving peace. Clearly the British, like the Americans in Vietnam or the Russians in Afghanistan, would like to be free of their entanglement, but losing even just this much of the Union was a bad precedent in the face of separatist movements in Scotland and Wales. The Irish Republic seemed little eager to absorb the troubled north. The Ulster Protestants were as intransigent as the Boers had been in South Africa. And given Sinn Fein's minority status as a political party even in Catholic areas, it was not likely that Gerry Adams would be accorded the same status as Nelson Mandela or Yasser Arafat. In my mind it kept coming back to whether those who would not have a monopoly on power could be interested in the concessions that must be made for peace.

At the same time Adams seemed to hold the best last hope for a diplomatic resolution. He was just enough older than those of Martin and Thomas's generation to remember that Northern Ireland had not always had the appearance of an occupied country. If he failed, the question was whether a new IRA, armed now even more formidably, would push for an entirely miltary solution even if this called for a guerrilla war lasting another twenty-five years.

I had many questions to ask Adams if the opportunity came to interview him as well. Just one was how he felt about his chances of living a long life. He had already been wounded in an assassination attempt in Belfast. If he succeeded in an arrangement less agreeable to many others in the IRA, might he face the same fate as Michael Collins, the legendary IRA leader killed because of his acceptance of partition? If he failed, could he avoid being hunted down by those on the other side?

SAN FRANCISCO: JANUARY 1996

Even though my parents were Irish, the fact that they had divorced when I was a toddler meant that I was not raised with the same sense of family as most of the people I was interviewing. For Thomas, the only unmarried child in his own family and someone who felt an obligation to work hard in the United States in order to send money to his relatives in County Fermanaugh, it seemed perfectly natural to see the relationship of brothers and sisters as the paradigm of loyalty. As my meetings with the San Francisco community proceeded, I began to sense how much this paradigm was a key to the sense of Irish Catholic identity that had allowed the IRA to succeed so well in its long guerrilla war.

The Irish experience is first of all rooted in the harsh land itself. Despite its awesome beauty, Ireland is an island with only limited uses for its land, particularly in the damp north. Cows, pigs, and goats were the key to wealth from an early period, as reflected in the tales of the cattle-rustling Ulster hero Cuchulainn, and it was as much to feed their pigs as themselves that the Irish came to rely so heavily on potatoes when this crop was introduced very early in the seventeenth century. In the north oats, rye, barley, and flax were dominant crops. The value of the grains in part depended on the extent to which they were allowed to be fermented and distilled, and the value of flax on the vagaries of the linen trade. Despite the richness of the ocean, the Irish did not take enthusiastically to fish in their diet: the Catholic practice of eating fish on Friday and in Lent was considered appropriately penitential.

The emphasis on grain and cattle allowed starvation to become an accepted means of war against the Irish from Elizabethan days, since burning the fields and killing the animals was much easier than slogging through the fens in pursuit of an enemy band. What other men did not do, nature itself often enough would, and prolonged bad weather was also a frequent cause of famine. And then, assuming a dominant place in the Irish imagination as the tale of how English callousness compounded a natural disaster, there was the blight that destroyed the potato crops in the 1840s and thus triggered the Great Famine that drastically reduced the island's population through starvation and emigration. It was not that the London government did nothing at all for the suffering people of what was supposedly part of the United Kingdom, but that it could not or would not do enough.

In Ireland as elsewhere, it is those with less of this world's goods who tend to have the largest families. It always seems counterintuitive that those who are the poorest should deliberately have the most children, yet the logic of it is simple enough, even apart from the idea that it provides a hedge against a high rate of mortality. There are more hands to do what work there is, and with more children, parents increase their chances of everyone benefiting from the success of a lucky few. There is little reason to restrict the size of a family and considerable reason to do the opposite. For this reason, Church opposition to birth control is probably not as significant a factor as it is sometimes made out to be, and the Irish would have been prolific even if the Vatican had decided early on to emulate the family planning of the People's Republic of China.

With too little arable land available for a new family to set up an independent household, the Irish pattern early on was that of delayed marriage for both men and women. Consequently, Irish offspring were spending more of their early adult years with their numerous siblings than would have been the case elsewhere, and the bonds of adolescence were not as readily broken. In a situation of perceived oppression, these bonds took on even stronger signficance.

Also, as Roddy Doyle shows in his novel *The Snapper*, about an Irish father dealing with his daughter's pregnancy, the English concern with respectability that fuels the work of Jane Austen and Charles Dickens as well as all the Merchant-Ivory period films, simply does not connect with an Irish mentality. Even the classic images of Catholic guilt—especially the supposed fear of sex that is cited in the denunciations of American Catholic school graduates turned angry young authors—is more part of an American experience of immigrants being indoctrinated with new standards of propriety. James Joyce, after all, was a Dubliner, and it was the English and the Americans who did not know what to make of him.

Put these two things together—the concern with family bonds and a proletarian disdain for what the neighbors might think—and the ability of an IRA man to avoid the stigma that might have been expected because of his activities is much more understandable. Martin's comment that "we are all volunteers" had been staying with me from the time we had met, and I became far more attuned to its significance when my wife and I accompanied our son to the annual dinner dance put on by Noraid at the Irish Cultural Center.

The year before, there had been ceremonies in the Bay Area to honor Jimmy Smyth and the three other escapees from the Maze. This year Mayor Willie Brown, who made the front page of the *Irish Times* for supporting a boycott of the Bushmill's distillery for its allegedly anti-Catholic hiring policy, was on hand to present proclamations to Mary Casey and Charlie Laverty, two long-time Noraid supporters. Jimmy Smyth was there, and both Thomas and Martin were highly visible.

I had a chance to introduce myself to Jimmy Smyth and Jennifer Pearse, and both indicated they were willing to talk more with me about their experiences. This I thought important for two reasons. The first was that the status of the IRA prisoners still in custody in England or Ireland was allowing a focus for expatriate activism comparable to the significance of the Americans held in Iran or in Vietnam some years back. The second was that it put a more human face on those from their own side while simultaneously stripping it from the enemy.

At our table I had a chance to talk with several men involved in Irish-American activism. One told me about his trips to the Falls Road area of Belfast well before the cease-fire and suggested some places to see when I went there. Another, whose wife surprised me by having a deeply personal interest in the Irish witch lore, which had been one of my research subjects for a book, gave me the name of a cousin serving a life sentence in the Maze. I wondered what stories I might have had from any of the several hundred others attending this function. Even if Martin's phrase "we are all volunteers" was a bit of hyperbole, the point was that there was a pervasive sense of family here. And this meant there would be a corresponding sense of loyalty much stronger than what I would have expected.

The next day was the interview I had come up for. In keeping with my policy of protecting the identities of most of those agreeing to talk with me, I'll call him Brian McGuinness. We were sitting in a basement room while the rest of his clan assembled in the living room and dining room upstairs to watch the Super Bowl. He had been living in an area near Belfast during the Civil War in the early 1920s, and he could remember a time when the boys from his Catholic neighborhood played soccer with their rivals from local Protestant schools. "We got along well until the English soldiers came," he said, "and the Protestants and the Catholics would get along fine again if the soldiers just go away."

Brian still had strong feelings about the Irish Free State (the earlier label of the Irish Republic, still favored by those who question its legitimacy) and its error in accepting partition. This led me to ask him about the explicitly socialist policies that had been part of revolutionary rhetoric from then down until now. From what he knew of the mood in Ireland today, was there really that much interest in thoroughgoing economic reform—or was socialism a dead issue with the dissolution of the Soviet empire?

Brian answered simply that it was all a matter of jobs, but he told me how he had seen the Communist ideal—which he seemed to equate with socialism as we kept talking—as a failure at an early age. It was one of those marvelous stories. After coming to San Francisco he had become a liquor distributor.

One time I got this order for fifty-five cases of beer. So I went to the address, which was off Market in one of those side streets, and I found there was a room with all the Communist posters hanging up. Now this was going to be a really big meeting, I was told. So I took two cases of beer at a time up a flight of steps, then the tubs and the ice. The next day I go back to get my empties and my money, and I find they had only drunk a case and a half of beer, and they didn't even want to pay for that half a case that was left.

I'm tired from taking all the cases back down and I'm feeling pretty miserable, so I stop in a bar for a shot. Someone in there starts going on about how the Communists were going to save the world, and I told him that if they couldn't get enough men together to drink more than a case and a half of beer, then they weren't anything to take seriously.

It was Irish logic at its best. It also was another bit of confirmation for the thesis I had been formulating about the place of a sense of solidarity in the Irish mind. In what Brian had told me and in what I remembered from growing up in a strongly Irish parish, it was important to be seen and be counted. It was the reason for the St. Patrick's Day parades, such as the one in San Francisco for which Brian had been a grand marshal a few years before, even though there were those who shouted at him that he was a terrorist because of his support of the republican cause.

In Dublin I had joked with my wife about the limited gene pool. What I had not then appreciated was that there was a psychological equivalent. In England it is standard to have local eccentrics, and oddball associations flourish readily. In the United States, as in France and Japan, there are exotic cults that run the gamut from silly but innocuous Elvis Presley churches to groups attempting mass murder. In Ireland such individualism, much less the fanaticism found in some groups, does not appear to exist. Whatever their reputation for extremism, even for gestures that are ultimately suicidal (with the abortive Easter uprising a prime example and the hunger strikes in the Maze arguably a more recent instance), groups such as the IRA and its rival INLA (the Irish National Liberation Army) do not move appreciably beyond an outlook characterizing wide segments of the general population. The Marxist concept of a revolutionary elite—a vanguard of the proletariat leading the masses to a place they are not yet able to envision for themselves—is alien in a society that is essentially rural and still not industrialized according to the standards found elsewhere.

Another way of seeing this is to look at the factors that do seem to be present in order to have groups such as the Symbionese Liberation Army that kidnapped and "brainwashed" heiress Patricia Hearst, or the Order of the Solar Temple that made headlines in France and Switzerland with its two sets of murder-suicides. The first is that there has to be a setting that allows both a high degree of individual alienation and sufficient personal anonymity for groups such as these to assemble. The second is that the established value system has to be sufficiently fractured, either because of the survival of an older scheme or because of exposure to an alien scheme, for a counterpoint to be significant. Both conditions exist in a cosmopolitan setting, which is not what characterizes Ireland.

The key point here is that despite the Anglo-Irish order that governed the entire island, the English assumption of racial superiority over besotted and belligerent Celtic brutes guaranteed an Irish consensus of victimization. The Great Famine, which disrupted any sense of the familiar, permitted a more desperate type of resistance to emerge, but in this respect the early Fenians and their IRA successors would not differ that much from the maquis of Nazi-occupied France and the partisans of Greece and Yugoslavia. Community support becomes a crucial factor—and it is not simply the fear of retaliation that inhibits informers but the perception that those engaged in violent resistance are entirely justified.

SAN FRANCISCO: FEBRUARY 1996

In the middle of February I returned to San Francisco after spending a weekend in Santa Cruz with other California ex-Jesuits at an annual retreat. I had been given much to pray about when on February 9 the IRA called off its eighteen-month cease-fire and an hour later detonated a powerful car bomb in the Dockside area of London. Just that morning I had contacted my editor to tell him I had been in contact with my guide in Northern Ireland, one of Thomas's close friends and a prominent Sinn Fein official in County Tyrone. I had joked about hoping the cease-fire would hold, since I had no training as a war correspondent. Only hours later I realized I might well be going into a war zone at that.

In only one way I could say this was good news: it would make for a much more interesting set of photographs.

My young friend Kevin was on the phone that evening. Thomas was already trying to learn what he could from his homeland. Hours later he relayed the information that the bombing had been ordered from the highest level of the IRA. For better or worse, it was not the action of a splinter group. The question was where this left Gerry Adams. If he had known and approved of the bombing, his credibility as a peacemaker was destroyed. If he had not known or could not have prevented it, it seemed his importance as a negotiator was destroyed.

In Santa Cruz I had spoken with a couple of ex-Jesuits with strong Irish links. One told me about his republican family in Monaghan, right on the border, and how the IRA used to set up ambushes for marauding British troopers. Inside the family closet, not visible to the casual visitor, there was a board covered with the Easter lily emblems sold to raise money for the IRA. And what about that older generation of volunteers? They were all dead or in prison.

My other Irish friend shuddered when I told him where I had been meeting some of those I interviewed. It was a noted "IRA bar"—one reason that three of the men being honored at a fund-raiser that weekend, escapees from the Maze who were fighting extradition, must not go there as a condition of their bond. "You can't solve anything with violence," he insisted. "They have to learn to pray." I was not bold enough to tell him that Thomas, who never missed Mass and lived an almost puritanical lifestyle, was also a man who kept insisting to Kevin that the Irish needed to set off a lot more bombs to force an English withdrawal.

On the way up to San Francisco I stopped at Jennifer Pearse's small house near the University of California at Berkeley. I found an attractive, ebullient young woman who was excited about her graduate studies and not at all bitter about her ruined career and the years she had lost in prison. I already knew some of the story—how she had been in contact with some young Irish nationals in the Boston area who were under close surveillance by the FBI. When one of the men interrupted an agent who was attempting to bug his car, there had to be a decision whether to abort the surveillance or make an arrest then. The FBI decided it was time to take them in—and then they came for Jennifer.

"I had no idea my phone had been tapped," she told me. "I could not believe I was being arrested."

At the time she was a recent graduate of San Francisco State with a degree in electrical engineering. She had found a good job in Silicon Valley—the first time she had ever had any money, she told me—and had not in any way thought her interest in republican activities could bring down the full wrath of the United States government. The charge was conspiracy to violate an obscure statute from early in the century that made it a federal crime to destroy property in a country friendly to the United States. The prosecution made the case that Jennifer, a novice engineer, was actively engaged in developing a sophisticated weapons system for the IRA, something she still found laughable. But she was convicted nonetheless, in part on the basis of items found in her possession, such as copies of *An Phoblacht*, the weekly republican newspaper published in Belfast.

I asked how her family had taken it. They were old-time leftists, she explained—the kind of people who came to expect FBI agents to be snooping into their lives. Jennifer herself had grown up in the tight-knit community of first-generation Irish-Americans in San Francisco. She had been in a group that was the Gaelic equivalent of the Girl Scouts, had played soccer on an Irish team, and had made many trips back to the country of her folks. One of her closest friends, as it turned out, had been the granddaughter of the man I've named Brian McGuinness whom I had interviewed just a month before. Everyone knew she was innocent and saw the trial as just another effort to intimidate anyone who expressed support for the cause of Irish freedom.

So how was prison life, I asked. Her surprising answer was that from the moment she arrived at the federal facility where she served most of her term, she had been taken in hand by a group of Puerto Rican women who were serving long sentences for their own actions against the American government. To them she was not a criminal but another political prisoner, and they made life as comfortable for her as they could. Also, she was close enough to San Francisco that her family and friends could come and visit easily, and she was never left to feel she had been abandoned.

The ordeal over, she had decided to enter a doctoral program at the University of California. Only a few people at the school knew what had happened—even the young man who was taking her across to San Francisco for the day had no idea he was dating a felon with supposed ties to a terrorist organization. "Maybe I'll tell him on the way over," she said. I promised not to blow her cover when I saw her later that evening.

3

Rule of the Redcoats

Northern England cannot stay Irish since it never was Irish. The six counties—Yorkshire, Lancashire, and so on—are, were, and always will be English. Import Irishmen from Dublin, Cork and Galway till they outnumber the native English by a 100 to 1, Northern England will remain stubbornly English. Otherwise, we would have to admit, would we not, that every thief who holds on long enough to his ill-gotten gains finally has a right to them?

Peter de Rosa, *Pope Patrick*

IRELAND: THE CENTURIES OF OCCUPATION

In his sardonic 1995 novel *Pope Patrick*, Peter de Rosa, who earlier had produced one of the most readable histories of the Easter rebellion, imagines a conversation between the newly elected pope, who is a somewhat unworldly Irish prelate, and the woman who is England's prime minister. In it Pope Patrick reverses the history of the two islands to imagine that it was England that had been occupied by Ireland in order to retell the story of contemporary "terrorism." The prime minister, of course, decides that he is thoroughly mad.

"Occupation," like "terrorism," is one of those words that takes its meaning from the user's politics. I once had a student who sat with a small Mexican flag on his desk to remind him, he said, that he lived in occupied Mexico. Another student, who was Sioux and Apache, had commented about an Indian friend who made much of the fact that he still saw Arizona and New Mexico—the area that the automobile club lists in its maps as Indian Country—as under foreign control. For the Catholic Irish in the northern counties, the sense of living in an occupied country depends on the degree of British military presence—and twice in this century that presence has been so overwhelming that it is difficult not to think of the area as one taken over by an invading enemy.

We could take all of this back to Henry VIII, who is arguably the first ruler to focus on developing a nation-state in our modern sense of the term. Before Henry it would not have been clear that sovereignty implied the dominance of the political order over everything else, especially religious institutions. Once Henry declared himself head of the Church of England, he not only appropriated the wealth of the bishops and abbots but also effectively ended any internal challenge to his authority. It was not surprising that his great-grand-nephew, James I, the Scots king who ascended the throne of England after the death of the woman who had executed his mother, took for granted that his rule was by divine right. James's son, Charles I, pursued this notion to his death, refusing to acknowledge the legitimacy of any English tribunal to put him on trial simply for importing French troops to enforce his claims.

The Irish people suffered under Elizabeth and then under Cromwell, the Puritan leader who refused the title and trappings of a monarch after the civil war that ended in the execution of Charles I. For Elizabeth there may not have been much difference between a visiting Indian chief from America and a visiting Irish lord such as Shane O'Neill, who addressed the court in Gaelic and punctuated his speech with howls. It was obvious that good Englishmen should rule over savages, but second best was to have compliant savages rule in England's name. In 1562 O'Neill was confirmed by the queen as "captain" of Tyrone, but the brutality of the manner in which he attempted to secure his hold over his fellow Irish invited them to ask for English assistance. A dozen years after his return to Ireland, O'Neill was challenged by the equally brutal Earl of Essex, Walter Devereux, now made governor of Ulster.

One ambitious English lord, Sir Thomas Smith, had already failed to establish what in effect was an English colony after promising to expel all Irish except for those who would work the soil for their English masters and never dare wear English clothing or carry a weapon. In 1574 Essex, whose tactics borrowed from one of the more sordid episodes in Scottish history, massacred his hosts after several days of banqueting in Dublin Castle, then the next year attacked a Scottish stronghold on

Rathlin Island in the North Channel and allowed his troops to butcher the garrison after accepting its surrender with the promise to spare the lives of the defenders. He still failed to secure the hold he had promised his queen, and he returned to Dublin with the title of earl marshal of Ireland but no further royal support.

Scots played a major role in the tangled politics of northeast Ireland for a number of years afterward. These were Catholic Scots, however, and the fear of an alliance of French and Irish and Scots against the English motivated Elizabeth to renew her efforts to take back the north. For a while, with the proclamation of Hugh O'Neill as Earl of Tyrone in 1585, it seemed she would be successful, but ten years later, having already failed to support the English cause at the siege of Enniskillen, O'Neill engaged in open combat with English forces. Following the precedent of Shane O'Neill, he also began recruiting Irish peasants and soon had a fully trained and equipped army that no longer had need of foreign mercenaries.

In 1601, Ulster forces, as Catholics helping Catholics, marched to the rescue of a trapped Spanish garrison at the south of the island, at Kinsale in southern County Cork. This time, though, the northerners were not fighting in familiar territory and were outclassed by the English army under Mountjoy.

Mountjoy pursued O'Neill north. His tactics involved starving his enemy by destroying crops and cattle, but this meant that there could be no distinction between soldier and civilian. Possibly he felt somewhat justified by the fact that the Irish had come to disregard the earlier conventions that made wars a contest between bands of professionals who could easily shift allegiance, depending on the resources of a would-be paymaster. What was effectively a policy of genocide now determined English actions, and the results were devastating; famine brought on horrific incidents of cannibalism. What has been called the Nine Years War ended in 1603 with Hugh O'Neill pardoned and feted in London, to the consternation of English speculators who had footed the bills for the war in the hope of sharing in the spoils.

James I, the theologically minded Scot whose twin fears of regicide and witchcraft inspired Shakepeare's production of *Macbeth*, was now the king. As the years went on, the Earl of Tyrone found himself with more troubles at home that included one chieftain, his son-in-law, rejecting both the marriage and the earl's overlordship. Things worsened when other nobles defected to Spain, and O'Neill, who was being summoned to England to settle the dispute over his daughter's marriage, realized that he, too, would be under suspicion and might find himself in the Tower. He left Ireland for Europe and eventually died in Rome, an exile who found that no European power was willing to challenge Britain in order to restore him to his lands.

An English plantation had been established in Monaghan in 1593. After O'Neill's flight, most of Ulster was decreed to be under the king's control, to be awarded to his loyal subjects. For James this was an opportunity to establish Protestant Christianity in an area "almost lost in superstition," as he put it. In 1610 the conditions were spelled out for applicants who would settle in Ulster. These so-called undertakers had to have taken the Oath of Supremacy and would agree to clear their estates of the native Irish. Ulster, like Virginia, was a colony, but it had the marked advantage of being on the same side of the Atlantic and thus had tremendous appeal to people in both Scotland and England who saw a chance to make their fortune. Apart from some Irish landowners prominent enough to be allowed to remain in place, the Catholic Gaels were on a par with the heathen Indians.

One difference, however, was that the Ulster colonists for the most part were not about to be field hands—and unlike America, there were no Africans to be bought as slaves. Whatever the king's intentions, the Irish stayed on the land from which they were to have been removed. All that had happened was that the rents they paid were higher and those to whom they paid them were individuals who spoke a different language and held a different religion.

Under Charles I, who came to the throne in 1625, there was not the same enthusiasm for subsidizing the English presence in Ulster. Instead, the provincials found themselves subject to increasing taxes and then, as Puritan opposition to Charles intensified in Scotland, English generals set about compelling the Scots in Ulster to take the so-called Black Oath, the rejection of the covenant that many had signed to oppose the new prayer book. In 1641 the Catholic lords of Ireland rose up in rebellion, and in Ulster this translated into a massacre of the Protestant settlers.

The war that followed was fully as brutal as anything that had happened a half-century before, and the English Civil War that began in 1642 complicated the situation even more. Charles was executed for treason at the beginning of 1649, and Oliver Cromwell, now Lord Protector, arrived in Ulster in the summer. His retaliation for the massacre of 1641 was to kill the soldiers he captured, even though most of them were English rather than Irish. Within a few years Cromwell's subjugation of Ireland was complete, and there were no great Catholic landowners left. The Restoration put an end to the more extreme efforts to enforce Protestant conversions, with the result that by 1685, when a Catholic again sat on the throne of England, Protestants found themselves in the position of being a dominant minority. Three years later James II was attempting to recover his throne after being replaced by William of Orange in the Glorious Revolution. The final failure of his efforts was at the Battle of the Boyne in 1690, when combined Protestant forces from all over Europe defeated a Catholic army essentially supported by France.

The Treaty of Limerick in 1691 did not explicitly ban the Catholic religion, but in the process of its ratification any effort to maintain the same freedom that had existed under Charles II was lost. The Protestant Ascendancy had begun. R. F. Foster writes in his *Modern Ireland* that those who were descended from settler gentry "asserted their ascendancy in a polity that had the status of a dependent kingdom, but psychologically and pragmatically partook of attitudes best called colonial." Ireland was now "the province"—but those who lived there were like their American cousins in finding that this implied some limitations on the concept of what it meant to be a full British citizen.

The Dutch William's victory with his Danish allies effectively ended an era in which Ireland, like Scotland in the Elizabethan period, had become linked with France, just as in the time of Hugh O'Neill it had attempted a link with Spain. Now the issue was whether there was any longer a specifically Irish nation. Differences of class read as differences in religion—gentry throughout the island and emerging capitalists in the Belfast area would be Protestant, and farmers and laborers would be Catholic. Gaelic would be proscribed in Ireland just as Welsh was in the southwest of England, and the future of the island would be in the hands of those who spoke English, looked to Canterbury rather than Rome, and saw London rather than Dublin as the seat of government.

BELFAST AND LONDON: MARCH 1996

Nine months earlier I had come to Dublin with an unreal image of what a Catholic city would look like. Now I was coming to Belfast with what turned out to be equally unreal expectations of a Protestant city defending itself against Catholic separatists. Apart from the perfunctory checkpoint on the road leading to the airport, I saw barely any indication of the British military presence. What was more surprising was that it would be several days before I saw my first Ulster constable. Despite the end of the cease-fire and the several incidents of IRA activity in London, Belfast remained quiet and almost insouciant. A cabdriver responded to my comment that I had expected more of a war zone by saying that only the bad news made the newspapers.

The city itself, settled in the seventeenth century but not really built up until the 1800s, lacked the sense of history of Dublin, which reached back to Viking times. There were not the massive cathedrals from an earlier age of faith, and many of the great stone buildings that from the outside looked to be places of worship turned out to have been converted into shopping centers. Even Queen's University had as many modern concrete and glass buildings as it did grand brick ones. The serrated housing tracts outside the commercial center, rebuilt after the German bombing of the Second World War and again after the massive destruction of the early years of the Troubles, were far more appealing than what I saw in either Dublin or London—and they were clearly more charming than the warrens of subsidized housing in American cities.

I had come with several purposes. Since I had been granted a week away from my classes to learn something more about overseas educational advances, I had scheduled meetings with faculty both at Queen's and at several of the colleges comprising the University of London. I also hoped to meet with some of the people in Sinn Fein, but as it happened, my key contact phoned me at the hotel and apologized for the fact that he was just then being sent by the party to Italy. What concerned him was that Thomas would think less of him for it. What mattered most to me, however, was having a chance to walk these streets and test their mood for myself.

Most striking to someone from Los Angeles was the remarkable Irish courtesy, a genuine interest in being helpful. For example, my wife and I might just be standing at a corner and asking each other about directions when someone nearby would cheerfully volunteer the information we needed. Extraordinary hospitality to travelers has always been remarked as a characteristic of Ireland, just as rudeness is to be expected by the tourist in France, and we were particularly reassured that the end of the cease-fire had not brought on the type of anxiety that made every stranger suspect.

I was still uneasy, however, when I set off on foot for the Falls, where I had an appointment with Father Sevan Timoney, the superior of the small Jesuit community in Belfast. Just a few years before, when the Falls was a "no-go zone," masked IRA patrols might have asked me my business. Even my Cadogan guidebook, published in 1995, advised me that "the [republican] communities are closed to strangers" and suggested it would not be wise "to walk about these parts at night." I relied on the fact that it was midmorning and I had enough of an Irish look about me that people might think I belonged.

I soon found my way to St. Peter's Cathedral, across the square from a burned-out church. I asked someone passing by whether the ruined church, which I thought I might photograph for this book, had been destroyed in the Troubles. No, I was told, it had burned down just a few weeks before, probably set afire by some mischievous kids. I stopped in St. Peter's and offered a prayer, on the theory that it couldn't hurt, then I asked a man coaching a group of boys playing soccer for directions to Antrim Road and the street I needed. He advised me to take a private taxi at an office next to a pub just a few blocks away.

Already I had heard about the black taxis that remain a basic means of transportation in the Falls, but this was my first experience with the unmarked cars that were the private cabs. Bravely, I walked into a smoke-filled room where a group of men who, for all I knew, donned balaclavas and cradled Armalite rifles in their spare time were waiting for fares. Someone knew the street I wanted, and for a couple of pounds cheerfully deposited me in front of a building that had no clear indication of being the residence of a group of priests.

Father Timoney himself, comfortable in slacks and a pullover sweater, was the type of Jesuit I had once aspired to be—urbane, learned, approachable. He accepted me immediately as someone to whom he would not have to explain the often unique terminology of the Jesuit order, and we talked easily about what was happening in the northern counties. Above all, he insisted, I needed to understand the complexity of the situation. "Fundamentalists" on both sides reduced everything to myths and slogans, with loyalists seeing only a conflict between Catholics and Protestants, and republicans seeing only a conflict between the Irish and the English.

I had already come to realize that religious differences were not that significant for the IRA and its supporters within Sinn Fein, most of whom had very limited affection for the Church that had repeatedly counseled an acceptance of the status quo. There were no Catholic counterparts to the ranting Presbyterian minister Ian Paisley, for instance—no priests who took either to the pulpit or to the barricades. The clergy, shrinking in numbers in Ireland, as in the United States, saw themselves not as rebels but as peacemakers, although it was obvious that their ecumenical overtures had not led

Paisley to back off from his quite colorful tirades against the Church of Rome.

I was slowly beginning to appreciate how much a political vision replaced a lost faith. In San Francisco I had gained some insight into the sentiments of the Irish émigrés, and repeatedly I heard that the Brits were the problem, as though when England once and for all agreed to give back the six counties, the kingdom of heaven would truly have arrived. Quoting Cardinal O'Faigh, Father Timoney remarked that ninety percent of the religious bigotry appeared on the loyalist side while ninety percent of the political bigotry appeared with the republicans. So far I had seen nothing with which to gainsay him.

Certainly I did not have a sense of being in an occupied country, even as I trudged through the Falls. Not that long ago there would have been the daily routine of nervous troopers facing off against angry residents, but now the military were all but invisible, restricted to their barracks but presumably ready to be deployed as necessary. What was evident was that the central city could be closed off to vehicular traffic in an instant. Father Timoney told me what it was like before the cease-fire, when at times the thick metal gates would be swung shut and all plans about either going out of the Falls or going back in would be put on hold. A tour bus driver added still another story of how at one time the Falls had been completely sealed off for several days because of a report of a cache of explosives, and in that short a period eighty members of the IRA had become eight hundred. I realized that with the cease-fire ended, the British authorities were avoiding any kind of high-profile activity that would be likely to provoke an incident—or restore some luster to the IRA after the incidents in London, which now included one of their own men blown up by a bomb he was carrying. If this was a gamble, it appeared to be paying off.

One thing that I did notice when, a few days later, I made my way to Queen's was that even central Belfast was slowly taking on a more distinctively Irish identity. I heard Irish spoken on the streets, saw Gaelic signs posted around the campus, and noted the manner in which Dublin rather than London was becoming the city with which to identify. Some things were trivial but instructive, such as the underground campaign to stick decals reading BRUSCAR, the Irish for "trash," on the litter boxes on the street. Other things were quite significant: Catholics now made up half the student body at the university, the Irish language was part of the curriculum, and even in Belfast there was an official *gaeltaght*, a public housing development available only to those fluent in the Irish language who would commit themselves to its use.

Over a steaming mug of coffee I asked one of the professors at Queen's about what difference it would make to have a central government just down the road in Dublin rather than across the sea in London. The economy would be worse, he thought, but beyond that it was hard to tell. As he spoke, I found myself wondering just what it was that I saw happening here. The northern counties, both before and after the founding of the Republic, had been the neglected stepchildren in the British Empire, so often struggling for recognition through an exaggerated expression of loyalty to the Crown and yet bemoaned as a constant source of anxiety and expense. Perhaps, as time went on, there would not be the cataclysmic battle for sectarian supremacy so often predicted, but a mutual assimilation in which Irish-speaking Protestants and unchurched Catholics would create a distinctive Ulster identity.

We did take a full tour of the city, from the historic shipyards that had seen the building of the *Titanic* to the sprawling suburbs that were attracting Catholics and Protestants to live side by side again. It was a Sunday, and barely anyone was on the streets in the central area. Only the American fast-food chains were open, and I had a cup of hot chocolate in a McDonald's while waiting to see if indeed there would be a tour bus operating that day. We were in luck, and I followed my wife to the top of an enclosed double-decker and sat happily at the front for the best view in the house.

The final part of the tour was through the two areas that were so well known by reputation to anyone who had read much about the Troubles. I had already been through part of the Falls, but this was my chance to see the entire section. Then we went through the Shankill, which was the literal stone's throw away from the Falls but separated from it by a so-called peace wall, a surprisingly ornate biscuit-colored stone structure bordered with thick shrubbery. Here, as elsewhere in clearly Protestant areas, there were large wall paintings of the IRA's deadly antagonists, the various loyalist paramilitary groups. In the Falls there were paintings also, most notably the mural of hunger-striker Bobby Sands on the wall of the Sinn Fein bookstore, but either the Catholics were not as good artists or there were simply more Protestant gunmen clamoring for public recognition. The bus driver went out of his way to point out that the presence of these elaborate graffiti should not be taken to indicate the true feelings of the local residents, and I thought of the various areas of Los Angeles in which local gangs announced their presence in a much less artistic manner. At home I knew a home owner might be taking his life in his hands to paint over graffiti, and I imagined that was even more true here.

Someone asked the driver how safe any of these areas were. Sensibly, he pointed out that he would not be driving through them if he felt there was the slightest danger. Again I thought of my own city, where the risk of being shot by a callous teenager at any time of the day was always on someone's mind. I remembered, too, that it was a young man from Belfast who had been shot while waiting for a bus in downtown New Orleans when I was there the previous summer. At least in the north of Ireland there was a reason for a shooting, which might be small comfort to the one shot but at least some reassurance that the city had not gone entirely mad.

I left Belfast without talking at length to anyone connected with Sinn Fein or the IRA. Although I had announced myself at the Sinn Fein bookstore and left a message for one of the people I had been told to contact, I did not get a call back, and later on the news I saw that the leading Belfast members of the party had been involved in a highly publicized effort to gain admission to the opening round of talks from which Sinn Fein had been excluded because of IRA actions. They were busy enough, and I was less eager to hear more of the party line at a time when the key figures in Sinn Fein were attempting almost desperately to insulate themselves from the public outrage at the latest IRA bombings. I knew I would have to return for a much more leisurely trip, but I had already accomplished something important in getting a better vision of what the north of Ireland was all about.

From Belfast we went on to London, where I had interviews arranged at several colleges for my work on Internet teaching. After the quiet streets of Belfast, virtually deserted at night, I had some difficulty readjusting to the constant press of humanity in the British capital. Here in this most cosmopolitan of cities I saw passersby in traditional African or Indian garb, heard numerous dialects, and was again made aware of how so many nationalities could be at home here. Oddly, though, I saw or heard nothing of the Irish language, and I began to think of what it must have been like for young Eddie O'Brien, the County Wexford man who had spent his last months in virtual seclusion in London while awaiting the orders that led to his death in a double-decker bus in the theater district.

A local newspaper contained an article about the Irish who came to London and pointed out how they filled only the most menial jobs. There were many Eddie O'Briens, anonymous visitors who would be marked by their accent and looked down upon accordingly, regardless of whether they were Protestants or Catholics, loyalists or republicans. For this particular visitor, though, there would be a mission, although not one that was intended to result in his death. Would it have concerned him, though, that some of his London neighbors might be injured or killed, or that there might be a drastic disruption of services, or that some important landmark might be reduced to rubble? As he listened to his stereo or watched programs on the telly, I imagine how the resentment grew, how his republican faith deepened, how the orders from someone he might never have met would seem a release from purgatory even while they set up a descent to hell.

How significant was it that Eddie O'Brien was not from the north, and not even from a republican family in the south? He was not one of those hard men who had killed and risked being killed in the gun battles of Belfast or Derry or Armagh. He had never been shoved against a wall by a British trooper, much less interned in a place like Long Kesh. There was not, then, the basis for a personal hatred that brought him to London. Instead there was only a republican faith made stronger by the fact that to the outside world it seemed so pointless. Consequently, holed up in a London apartment, he needed to believe in the IRA and its cause, because otherwise he was just another worthless Irishman in a city seemingly oblivious to the cause of Irish freedom.

I wondered what were the alternatives. In the absence of full debate it is easy enough to imagine that attention can be summoned through a dramatic piece of violence. One thing did seem true enough: British television and the major newspapers, which are national rather than local, were far more interested in the tangled relationship of Charles and Diana than they were in events in "the province." Ireland, even that bit of it to which England still laid claim, could just as easily have been across an ocean, too distant to be of any great concern. Maybe this was only to be expected. After all, how much coverage did an American paper or an American network give to events in Puerto Rico?

Still, I was surprised to see that there was far more of an Australian presence in London than there was an Irish one of any kind. I had some five-pound notes from Belfast, which unlike American currency are issued by local banks. The driver of the airport bus thought at first a note from the most prominent bank in Ulster had been issued in Scotland, and then a cabdriver flatly told me that I could not use another five-pound note, probably because there was not a picture of the queen on the front. At a currency exchange booth I traded in the offending bill, although the man there said that, if he followed company policy, he should not be taking it. Even a staunch Belfast loyalist might have been taken aback at this evidence of some lack of unity within the United Kingdom. For myself, I was beginning to root for a common European Union currency.

SAN FRANCISCO: APRIL 1996

I came up to San Francisco for a very specific purpose—to take part in the commemoration to be held at Holy Cross Cemetery in Colma, just south of the city. By this time I was far more familiar with republican customs, and one of the most important was the annual celebration of the Easter Uprising of 1916. On the eightieth anniversary and at a time when the IRA seemed adamant about continuing its war against the British, I was curious just what would be said.

Shortly before noontime a fife and drum band, whose members included both young children with tin whistles and adults with large drums, fell in behind a group of green-shirted flag bearers with both the Stars and Stripes and the Tricolor, followed by the flags of the four original Irish provinces, including Ulster. There were maybe four-score more of us, all true republicans with paper Easter lilies and green ribbons pinned to our coats, who marched behind to the grave of a turn-of-the-century Irishman, Thomas Esmond, whose place in the republican pantheon had been earned by assisting in the jail-break of a group of Fenian prisoners held in Australia.

There were anthems and a ballad of the woman with four fields, her jewels, taken by strangers until her brave sons, through the spilling of their blood, recovered all but one, and now the sons of those sons would fight to recover the last. A key part of the ceremony involved laying wreaths, and with almost avuncular pride I watched Jennifer Pearse, herself introduced as an Irish political prisoner, lay down a wreath on behalf of all the prisoners, then step back with a smart military salute.

Then there were the speeches. One was by Bernadette O'Hagan, a charming lady one might have expected to find behind the counter of a little shop in some tourist trap. The mother of two sons interned by British, she had herself been in the women's prison in Armagh. The other speech was by John Henning, a former ambassador and a respected labor leader, who bluntly reminded us that we were here to honor the fallen members of the IRA, the most recent of whom was Eddie O'Brien. The war had been taken to London, he said, and the

IRA should not give up its weapons until the last British soldier was gone. It was by far the most blunt statement of identification with the IRA that I had yet heard in any of the time I had spent in San Francisco, and it gave the lie to the statement that the IRA was simply an extremist group cut off from the people it had sworn to defend.

I was reminded of a satirical column that had appeared in a Galway newspaper. In it the author talks about coming across a would-be IRA liberator, garbed in a black balaclava and sporting a brightly polished Armalite, who is getting a drink in an Irish bar and cursing the people who fail to appreciate his efforts to save them, whether they want to be saved or not. That disdain for the IRA had been, I think, a common enough sentiment in the south, but here in the Bay Area I was among exiled northerners for whom the war was altogether too real as British troopers marched through their streets. They applauded the ambassador heartily.

The final address was the Easter greeting from the command of *Oglaigh na hEireann*—a salute to all of us who supported its struggle and, interestingly enough, a gesture of respect to Sinn Fein for its own efforts to work toward peace.

Later I attended a brunch with many of those who had been at the commemoration. It was a relaxed setting, and someone asked whether I had ever heard of Irish Alzheimer's. It was defined as the condition in which you forget everything except what you begrudge.

I talked a bit with one young Irishman about my impressions of Belfast, especially about how quiet it had seemed. He commented that the low-profile approach in the city was for the journalists. In the countryside, however, the British troops were making their presence known in a continuing campaign of intimidation. Well, I would be back soon enough to see for myself.

Part II

A Nation of Rebels

Regrettably, however, the fact that they might be regarded as international bandits never seemed to deter any of Britain's rulers from Henry II to Mrs. Thatcher from seizing and holding on to what they regarded to be in Britain's interest.

Jack O'Brien, *The Unionjacking of Ireland*

4

The Catholic Problem

You and that oul' eejit Paddy are pups from the same Fenian litter,
but you remember one thing, young fella-me-lad, yous may have
the music and songs and history and even the bloody mountains,
but we've got everything else; you remember that!

Gerry Adams, "The Mountains of Mourne"

In his marvelous short story "The Mountains of Mourne," Gerry
Adams describes a shouting match between a young Catholic who
has found a job helping deliver liquor over the Christmas season and
the slightly older Protestant with whom he has to work. Gradually
the two men have managed to establish a good rapport that is rup-
tured when, in the Mountains of Mourne near Belfast, they give a
ride to a drunken old man who expresses his thanks in Irish as they
drop him off. Geordie, the Protestant, feels immediately threatened,
all the more because he must agree that he, too, is affected by the
magic of the area with its lyrical Irish names.

"We've got everything else." It is too much a cliché to identify the
Protestants of the northern counties with the Boers of South Africa,
as though the self-styled Ulstermen are striving to maintain a dominant position to which they have no right. As Father Timoney had
insisted to me in the Falls, the situation was far more complex. Reviewing the history of the last four centuries, particularly the story of
the Ulster Plantation set up by James I, it is hard to say whether the

Protestants, especially those who did not belong to the established church, were not as much victims of events in London as the Catholics were. Throughout the British Isles those who identified with the austere views of John Calvin managed to give a political connotation to the words "dissident" and "nonconformist"—something all Americans are supposed to remember during the retelling each Thanksgiving of how the Pilgrims settled in New England, during the time of the Black Oath. Presbyterians were always suspect because of their rejection of the ecclesiastical hierarchy, which had not been abolished but only redirected during Henry's break with Rome, and in some ways they might be thought more dangerous than Catholics because of their wealth and prominence. The Catholic James II acted to suppress them in just the same way as his great-grandfather, the first James, attempted to suppress Catholics.

But this has been gross intolerance imposed from the outside. Within Ireland itself there is not the same record of religious bigotry, despite the sectarian rioting that has characterized Belfast in particular over the last two hundred years. My own suspicion is that this is because the people of Ireland are much less inclined to be fanatics about anything, religion included. Possibly it is the fact that as residents of a relatively small island with terrible weather, they are more interested in solidarity than in singularity. What extremist tendencies there are in religion might be traced to the rigid Augustinian outlook—especially the emphasis on predestination, personal unworthiness, and sexual repression—that shaped the Calvinism of the Scottish Protestants who emigrated to Ulster just as it shaped the Jansenism that dominated the French seminaries that trained Irish priests in the middle of the seventeeth century.

It may also be that fanaticism is an intellectual luxury that is simply out of place when so often survival itself has been in question. For instance, periods of starvation, whether the result of natural calamity or human decision, as in the various campaigns of the English invaders, do take the edge off fasting as a spiritual discipline. In the same way, sexual denial seems counterproductive when children can be so readily slaughtered.

This is a point I have made before, but it merits repeating as a counter to a great deal of nonsense about the mystical Irish soul as well as a tendency to interpret volunteers as secular martyrs pursuing a worldly equivalent of the priest's identification with the suffering Christ. There is, of course, an almost atavistic delight in the grand gesture—what almost does seem a throwback to the days of naked Celtic warriors charging heavily armored Roman troops—and Irish ballads constantly come back to the theme of bravely facing death, especially when it is death in pursuit of Irish freedom. But that is not at all the same as encouraging someone to be a suicide bomber or to engage in some grand campaign of extermination, neither of which has characterized events in the north despite fears that they could.

Protestants and Catholics have in general managed to coexist quite well. The exceptions—all too frequent in Belfast—are more clearly functions of group rivalry for a share of often very limited goods, such as jobs or housing. It is obviously coexistence rather than full integration, but in this century, especially at its end, coexistence alone seems increasingly an elusive goal, as is all too evident in the former Yugoslavia, in Russia, in Rwanda, in India, and possibly even in the United States with the rise of a strong white supremacist movement to parallel groups such as Minister Farrakhan's Nation of Islam.

As a young Jesuit, I had learned a fair amount about the repression of Catholics in the British Isles. As do most major religious orders, we had our own roster of saints celebrated with special feast days. Among them was Edmund Campion, a poet and a priest. In his youth he had been a skilled orator noted by Queen Elizabeth, and he had initially taken holy orders as a Protestant in Dublin. In 1573 he entered the Jesuits in France and was ordained five years later. In 1580 he was sent back to England to minister to Catholics while posing as a peddler. A year later he was arrested, tortured (permissible to extract confessions when the charge was treason), and executed. His defense that he was not lying to the officials who had initially asked him whether he was a priest was the "jesuitical" argument that he had engaged in a legitimate form of equivocation in his denial. I had a Jesuit professor who glossed Shakepeare's use of the term "equivocation" in the mouth of the drunken porter in *Macbeth* as a reference to this Catholic defense.

Catholics who refused to attend services of the Church of England were called "recusants"—a word that happily has now passed out of our usage except in those situations in which we hear of a judge being asked to recuse or disqualify himself from a trial. The point, of course, is that an Anglican, especially anyone who was "High Church," could hardly have accused a Catholic of heresy. Instead, someone who refused to get with the program and worship in the official church (which, after all, most likely was a building maintained by Catholics in a bygone era) was expressing a disrepect for the queen that, carried too far, would be interpreted as treason. Unlike the situation in Europe, where Catholics and Protestants alike enthusiastically attempted, in the name of God, to save the souls of heretics by burning their bodies, prayer was a clearly political act. People died not for insulting the divine Lord but for insulting His more worldly representatives.

The Tudor era has always fascinated me in the way violence could take on such an urbane character. Executions were public entertainment on Tower Hill, and those appointed to die for the edification of their countrymen were expected to tip the hooded man with the ax. Former prominence counted for nothing except perhaps to bring the execution inside castle walls. Henry lopped off the head of his former chancellor, Thomas More, as easily as he did the heads of two of his wives. Elizabeth decapitated her cousin Mary, even though she was the Scots queen, as well as some former favorites, including Robert Devereux, son of the Lord Essex who had attempted the conquest of Ireland. Repeatedly someone might gain a lasting acclaim—as did More and Mary and Edmund Campion—by cheerfully professing belief in a blissful immortality to be won in moments more, as though the executioner did them a favor by bringing them so quickly to paradise.

This, however, was perhaps a step forward from the days when the conflicts of knights representing either white or red roses meant everyone suffered. Those true celebrities who were executed, most typically with the suggestion that they conspired to dethrone their monarch and so plunge England back into fratricidal conflict, were like a new breed of sacrificial lamb. Their deaths ensured continuing youth and vitality to the regime, and more ordinary people could go on with their business, reassured that their monarch was not a soft-hearted threat to their security.

Catholics did, of course, represent a serious problem to the extent that those in power believed they could be manipulated by foreign influences. Like those accused of communism in the McCarthy era in the United States, the perception was that they were lacking in loyalty to the lawful government of their own country. Attending Anglican services seemed an almost trivial way to assure their neighbors that they were English first and Roman second, and their refusal could only strengthen the view that they were really Roman first. And there were plots, and there were unhinged individuals who might easily think themselves on a mission from God to purge England of the "heretical" queen. For the most part, though, England's first secret service, under Francis Walsingham, was ruthlessly efficient. Men such as Campion did not have a prayer of getting by without detection, and there were the tortures of the rack, designed to elicit detailed confessions that included the names of other conspirators.

The laws that were passed called for increasingly severe fines and forfeitures for absence from church, yet the evidence suggests that Catholics in England were not treated all that harshly. Many still held positions of power, and those with some experience of British politics could think it reasonable to hold out if they were Catholic or restrain themselves if they were not. After Henry's death there had again been a Catholic on the throne in the person of Mary Tudor ("Bloody Mary," who chopped off Protestant heads just as her father had chopped off Catholic ones), and who could say what would happen after Elizabeth's death or defeat? There was not to be another Catholic monarch until after the Civil War, however, but then years later James II proved unable to consolidate power, and those who had backed him were left to suffer the consequences.

In Ireland the consequences were considerable. Many Irish soldiers, the "wild geese," resorted to banditry for survival, and those Catholics not already dispossessed of their lands were now in effect internal exiles, not allowed to participate in any way in the government of the island. Gradually the harshest restrictions—such as the banishment of bishops and priests and forfeiture of inherited property—were eased, but by the end of the eighteenth century it remained illegal for a Catholic to enter the professions or to be politically active. Even intermarriage was prohibited. It was a situation in which the modern slogan "ballots, not bullets" would have seemed a cruel joke, since Catholics effectively had access to neither.

What is striking is how dissimilar the situations of English and Irish Catholics were. Both were politically restricted—something that meant far less in an age of limited suffrage than it would today—but there was no apartheid in England or Scotland, where someone born Catholic could easily put aside that identity, as there was in Ireland. Granted, the early talk of genocide and virtual serfdom had faded, and historians suggest that the restrictions on owning land actually contributed to the rise of a Catholic middle class that had to earn its living through commerce. However, the fact was that Catholics and Protestants would now be living apart with no chance to meld their cultures. Although a number of the old Irish Catholic aristocrats did "turn" to keep their lands in the family, someone less well born was expected to know his place and keep to it. The point was that Protestant landowners needed laborers whom poverty would keep dependent, and with the rise of industry in Belfast, there was to be the same visible ranking of jobs, with the easier and better-paying going to Protestants and the more onerous and lower-paying relegated to Catholics imported from the countryside.

Ireland, in other words, was like California and other states that
require unskilled foreign labor from Mexico, limit the chances for
anglicization, and then blame their economic woes on the exploding
population of Hispanics. During the Protestant Ascendancy, there
was a difference not just of religion but also of culture, and the so-
called Anglo-Irish had much in common with their colonial counterparts in America and then in India as they struggled with their
"white man's burden" over a people that they persisted in seeing as
racially distinct and therefore racially inferior. True, there were some
Protestants in Ireland who rediscovered a Gaelic culture that had
nearly ceased to exist, but this was not with the intent of making
themselves over as Gaels. They were the white men romanticizing a
savage culture just as other colonial writers romanticized American
Indians, and their vision of a Celtic twilight had just about as much
political sophistication.

Simple racism, then, is much more the key to the historical conflicts in Ireland than anything about whether the Lord's Supper was
celebrated in Latin according to the *Missale Romanum* or in English
according to the Book of Common Prayer. The Irish—who would be
depicted on English and American stages in much the same way as
blacks as loud, violent, intemperate, and fundamentally uneduca-
ble—were typically given simian features in political cartoons so as
to reinforce the notion of brutishness. Like Hispanics and American
blacks, they were seen as oversexed, as though superior physical en-
dowment was the natural compensation for being of lower intelligence, and consequently a danger to pure English women and a
fitting target for the sword or the whip of a proper English gentleman. Irish women, like black and Hispanic women, were seen as
readily promiscuous—suitable liaisons but never acceptable wives (a
theme that appears in the novel and film *A Circle of Friends*, about
the Ireland of just a generation back).

There were Anglo-Irish who did see a larger picture and so in
some way contributed to a new sense of Irish, contrasted with British, identity. Perhaps the most famous is Jonathan Swift, dean of St.
Patrick's Cathedral in Dublin, who satirized religious divisions within
Protestant ranks in *Gulliver's Travels* and assaulted Britain's Irish policy in his "Modest Proposal" (published just forty years after the Battle of the Boyne). Certainly the most important for Irish republicans
still is Wolfe Tone at the end of the eighteenth century. Swift, however, was no friend of the Catholics, and Wolfe Tone, well read in the
French deism that characterized the Paris revolutionaries who killed

their king at the same time they banned the Church, is characterized as seeing Catholicism as "a dying superstition."

Irish Catholics did regain the right to vote—but not to hold office—in legislation passed in Dublin in 1793 to mute the attractiveness of French radicalism. This did not prevent talk of insurrection, however, and in the following years tough new laws allowed a more vigorous prosecution of seditious politicizing. Reading how the British government continued to react to fears of the United Irishmen, predominantly Catholic for the simple reason that most people in Ireland outside of the northeast were Catholic, I find many of the same things characterizing British policy in the Troubles: suspension of normal habeas corpus laws, widespread political arrests, burning the houses of suspected radicals, the use of state-sanctioned terrorism and a corresponding failure to control British troopers, and official punishment for those in government who admitted to there being a problem in the way things were handled. Possibly I should be reassured by such evidence of British consistency over the centuries.

In what could have been a far more successful replay of what had happened a century before, the French Republic did attempt an invasion in 1796, with Wolfe Tone on board one of a fleet of forty-three ships. Because of bad weather and internal feuding, it never came off, but historian R. F. Foster refers to it as "a great might-have-been in Irish history." There was a revolution in 1798, beginning in Dublin and ending in Donegal, where Wolfe Tone was captured. It was a brutal affair in which thirty thousand died, and afterward the essentially colonial government of Ireland, which had worked through a parliament in Dublin, was moved to England, where an act of union between the two countries was passed in 1800.

Efforts at revolution were not squelched by this but only intensified. Orangemen were now unionists, and their Catholic adversaries continued to mobilize in a series of organizations, some directed to clearly political ends, such as complete Catholic emancipation—a right to full participation in British political life that would include holding office—and others once more aimed at attempting to free Ireland from all British control. This was the world of Daniel O'Connell and then of Charles Parnell, whose failures to bring about radical change through peaceful means offered a seeming justification for the Fenian movement.

In 1800 England had completed the action begun in Elizabeth's time. Ireland was part of "Great" Britain, swallowed up but not fully digested. Possibly, had there been a systematic effort to include the Irish in British national events, things could have worked out differently. However, this would have meant allowing Catholics to function fully as British citizens, and that still seemed unthinkable. So again there was a religious test and a painful reminder of second-class citizenship.

Once more we have to ask what was really troubling London—the religion of the Irish or the Irishness of those with that religion? My suspicion is that it was the simple fact of being Irish, and it would not have mattered that much had all the people of Ireland renounced the pope at once and switched to an Anglican liturgy. The Irish, like the Hispanics in my own country, would have still been the strangers even if they were coreligionists. They had been threatened with genocide and had survived, and that alone made them unwelcome. They prospered even when they had been deprived of what just a century before had been the sole source of wealth—their land. When the potatoes failed at midcentury and mass starvation thinned out the burgeoning population, I suspect that there was a subliminal sense of relief among the English. Just as there are those who see AIDS as God's curse on homosexuals, so the famine could be interpreted as God's curse on those who lacked the appropriate degree of loyalty to their monarch.

I doubt that this thought was ever expressed so baldly in public, but this was the era of Charles Dickens, in which poverty and wretchedness were seen, in a truly Calvinist spirit, as evidence of a predetermined damnation, just as worldly prosperity was a sign of election. It was also the era of Karl Marx and Friedrich Engels, who interpreted the role of "ideology" as a false consciousness obscuring the actual dynamics of human relationships, and there was a definite Victorian ideology that assumed Britain's right to rule over demonstrably inferior peoples. Ungrateful peoples, like ungrateful children, deserved to perish, and the Irish repeatedly withheld the appropriate degree of gratitude for having been allowed their state of dependency.

Damned because Catholic and Catholic because damned, Ireland barely survived the famine and the subsequent waves of emigration. The Elizabethan aspiration of having an island purged of the Irish, to be resettled by a better stock, might almost have been brought to reality. What did happen was that it was the Irish transplanted across the Atlantic who gradually ascended to the political heights denied their people in England. Militantly Catholic in a country that maintained the inherited English hostility toward the pope, the Irish moved from the Church Suffering to the Church Triumphant in a matter of generations. With their success here, the Irish in America could begin to take a greater interest in the fortunes of those they had left behind, both subsidizing their relatives and beginning a political pressure that would force an entrenched British establishment to rethink its options.

What was happening, however, was that the Church itself, so important to American Catholics, was becoming an obstacle to Irish independence. In the late nineteenth century, with the loss of a large land base in the so-called Roman states to the nation of Italy, the Catholic hierarchy had attempted a policy of consolidation that would give the Vatican a new sense of power. This was the period in which papal infallibility was defined as a dogma, not long after the pope had assaulted Protestant sensibilities by announcing as another article of faith that Mary had been conceived free of the taint of the original sin of Adam (which is what Catholics mean by "the Immaculate Conception," too often confused with the notion of Mary having conceived Jesus while still being a virgin). For a long while the Catholic Church, which in Elizabeth's time had fully deserved the scathing criticisms of Protestant reformers, seemed to be very successful in maintaining a picture of otherworldly dedication with its legions of priests and sisters, its affluent parish churches and thriving parish schools. Nowhere was this more true than in the United States, which relied on Irish-born clergy to sustain its growth.

In such a setting the Church had a strong interest in maintaining positive relationships with secular powers. The days when popes were linked with emperors were gone. The Vatican, which until Mussolini was a ministate under siege, cultivated goodwill everywhere, including England. What this meant for the Irish, whose intellectual leaders earlier in the nineteenth century had followed the inspiration of their freethinking French allies in their opposition to any organized religion, was a cultural split personality that continues to the present. On the one hand there is the reverence for Catholic piety, and on the other the blithe disregard for Catholic injunctions against belonging to "secret societies," such as the original Fenians had been and the IRA is today.

Much of the less frequently told story of revolution in both the United States and France involves the role of organizations that mimicked older Catholic orders in their use of quasi-religious rituals and secretive solemn professions. Freemasonry, with its roots in the occultist legends of the seventeenth century, emerged as a powerful international movement in the eighteenth century. Its main emphasis, compatible with Protestant views on personal inspiration, was on the role of a self-sufficient reason to accomplish human goals without the control of either a hierarchical church or an autocratic monarch.

Part of the oath-taking at the higher levels was sworn opposition to Rome. Understandably, Rome prohibited Catholics from being Masons, and those opposed to Catholics, such as the Ulster Protestants, were inspired to follow the Masonic pattern. The Orange Order was founded in Armagh in 1793 by members of a Protestant street gang, the Peep O'Day Boys, who were embroiled in bloody sectarian fighting with members of a Catholic street gang, the Defenders. To Orangemen, whose oath of loyalty to the king of England and his heirs was conditional on their support of the Protestant Ascendancy, it did not matter that the Dublin archbishop in 1795 excommunicated the Defenders, so that officially they were no longer really Catholic. Clearly the excommunication had no significance for the Defenders themselves.

What happened in the late eighteenth century set the pattern for the peculiar three-way split that has characterized the group relationships in Northern Ireland ever since. Protestants, definitely the minority in Ireland as a whole, equated religion and political power. Catholics, who lacked political power, did not and effectively could not equate it with religion. Instead, there would be the institutional church that attempted to remain apolitical, almost as though express loyalty to the Crown in civil matters would cancel any implication of disloyalty in the refusal to accept the Oath of Supremacy. And then there would be the revolutionaries, damned as Catholics regardless of whether they went to Mass or particularly respected the decisions of the Irish hierarchy. On both sides, Protestant and Catholic, the flash points would be where the working poor were forced to fight over limited opportunities, typically with the aggression coming from Protestants who felt threatened by Catholic incursions.

For Irish Protestants, then, the fact that theirs was a minority religion gave a lasting impetus to a battle against "popery," as though Rome was still a political power to be reckoned with. For Irish Catholics, excluded from full participation in the civic life of their own land, religious freedom was no longer an issue but political equality was. Just how that struggle was to be carried on—by strictly legal means or through violence—was what caused a deep but not usually visible division among Catholics themselves. The Tudor emphasis on religious uniformity had long ago burned itself out, and no Catholic had any reason to complain about impositions on his conscience in anything connected strictly with worship. The Church itself was comfortable with the arrangement, preferring to have its members focus on the Kingdom of Heaven and avoid any high degree of political activism in an age where an opposition to monarchy and anti-clericalism seemed to go hand in hand.

Beginning with the Armagh Defenders and continuing with the Fenian Brotherhood and then the IRA, Catholics convinced that political freedom and economic opportunity would come only with Irish independence had to deal with the fact that their priests and bishops had a vested interest in the status quo. It was in no way correct, then, to speak of a Catholic cause as though the rebels were fighting for their Church.

To Ulster Protestants, who already felt threatened enough, the political meekness of the Catholic hierarchy seemed clearly at odds with the statements that came from the Vatican—especially the late nineteenth-century condemnation of any "modernism" that insisted on a separation of church and state—and the new, highly emotional displays of public piety toward the Virgin Mary that inevitably played right to the traditional Protestant antagonism to anything that smacked of idolatry. In this they were not all that different from American Protestants, many of whom saw the separatist Catholic school system and the rising dominance of Irish Catholics in Democratic party politics as fearsome harbingers of a coming loss of freedom.

5

The Easter Uprising and Its Consequences

Yous are all nicely shanghaied now! Sorra mend th' lasses
that have been kissin' and cuddlin' their boys into th' sheddin'
of blood! . . . Fillin' their minds with fairy tales that had no
beginnin', but, please God,' 'll have a bloody quick endin'! . . .
Turnin' bitther into sweet, an' sweet into bitther. . . . Stabbin'
in th' back th' men that are dyin' in th' threnches for them!
                    Sean O'Casey, *The Plough and the Stars*

In O'Casey's mordant tribute to the Easter Rebellion, written a decade after the event, Bessie, a Protestant woman with a son at the
front, consistently mocks the pretensions of the men dressed in the
green uniforms of the Irish Citizen Army. At the end, when British
troopers come to the room where they believe they have shot a
sniper, hers is the body by the window. My wife and I saw the play in
London in 1995, after we had been in Dublin, and I had to keep
asking myself what was the subtext for this English audience. The
cease-fire was still on, so was the message to be that the last two
decades of violence were as senseless as the four days of violence
nearly eighty years before?

O'Casey himself had been caught up in the organization of the
Irish Citizen Army in 1913. Its very existence is one of those odd
features of the Irish scene at the time of the First World War. In the
area around Belfast the British military had actively assisted in the

gunrunning that armed the original Ulster Volunteers, even though there was the potential that these weapons might be turned against British soldiers called on to enforce any home rule order from Parliament. There was money and there were willing sources of supply—and it was soon obvious that those London politicians who saw the Ulster situation as a basis for running the Liberals out of power were making it clear that those northerners who saw themselves as English rather than Irish would not be held accountable for any illegal activities.

Nationalists did not have the same financial resources, and their own efforts at smuggling in whatever weapons they could buy were most often frustrated by the British police and military. In 1913, when the Irish Citizen Army was formed in Dublin in the wake of a bitter labor dispute, it was parading with broomsticks and taken not at all seriously by British authorities. The Irish Volunteers, linked with the banned Irish Republican Brotherhood, were not much better prepared to sustain a successful military campaign and, though closely watched, were not much feared. Above all, any effort to crack down on illegal weapons would have had to be directed first and foremost at influential Protestants in the north, so the fact that there were still a few firearms available to Catholics did not seem troublesome. In Ulster it would have been suicidal for nationalists to challenge armed Orangemen, and in the rest of Ireland it was still apparent that the British could respond quickly and decisively to a show of force.

When England entered the First World War the following year, Catholics as well as Protestants freely enlisted to fight for the Crown. For many it was a chance to have an income and a measure of respect as British troopers. For some it was also a gesture of loyalty that they hoped would be reciprocated when home rule was voted on again.

Those who saw England's troubles as Ireland's opportunity were definitely in the minority. The 1916 rebellion was the work of a small coterie of individuals who seemed unlikely revolutionaries. James Connolly was a labor leader who believed on ideological grounds that British capitalists would not destroy valuable property in Dublin. Patrick Pearse was a schoolmaster who probably had absorbed too much Hegel in his academic training and thus had a tragic tendency to exaggerate the significance of bloodshed in achieving a sense of national identity. Joseph Plunkett, already dying of tuberculosis even as he planned his wedding for that Easter Sunday, was a writer on the arts who interested himself in military strategy. Michael Joseph O'Rahilly, also a writer but also one of the founders of the

Irish Volunteers, was originally opposed to the rising and attempted to countermand it, yet he threw in his lot with the rebels once the fighting started. Thomas MacDonagh was a playwright and professor. Eamonn Ceannt was involved in athletics and music. Only Sean McDermott (MacDiarmada) and Thomas Clarke, who had been imprisoned fifteen years for an aborted bombing in London, fit the stereotype of the hardened revolutionary. Their principal support came from the exiled John Devoy, who was prominent in Clan Na Gael in the United States, and Roger Casement, a diplomat who had distinguished himself for his exposure of human rights violations in Africa and South America.

Casement had been smuggled into Germany with the intention of forming a brigade of Irish liberationists from among prisoners of war held by the Germans. The goal was to have these men return to Ireland, where, with German officers and artillery, they would free their island from British occupation. He severely underestimated the loyalty of the prisoners to their fellow fighting men. Those he did recruit were hardly worth the effort, and the Germans could not afford to spare their own elite officers or the type of equipment required for an uprising. They did agree to provide some rifles and ammunition, which would be sent to Ireland on a ship outfitted to pass as a Norwegian cargo ship. This plan went awry when the rebels decided to delay the landing but were unable to communicate the change to the commander of the German vessel, which was eventually forced to sail to England, where it was scuttled by its crew. Casement had already returned by German submarine; his own intention was to call off the uprising because he saw it as doomed to failure. He was captured not long after he had put ashore.

The uprising, originally planned for Easter Sunday, began the day following. Normally, in the Catholic calendar, it is the week before Easter that marks the time of suffering. This year it was to be the week after.

The rebels, about a thousand men, did take the General Post Office on Sackville Street (today O'Connell Street) in Dublin as well as a few other buildings. They managed to hold out four days before being forced to surrender, but in that period they saw their hopes completely frustrated when the impoverished Catholics of Dublin, rather than joining in the rebellion on the model of the Parisians who had stormed the Bastille, saw only an opportunity to loot the downtown stores. As they were marched through the streets, the rebels found themselves jeered by the people they had thought to liberate. What they had not counted on was that for so many Dubliners—the "separated" wives in particular—war had brought a measure of security with soldiers' benefits. Also, the idea of fighting against men who wore the same uniforms as their husbands and sons and brothers went completely against the popular mood.

It was then that the British command, which had taken over control from the civilian representatives of the Crown, managed to turn an almost farcical rebellion into the stuff of legend by deciding on the peremptory trial and execution of its leaders. All seven of those who signed the proclamation of the Irish Republic (Clarke, McDermott, MacDonagh, Pearse, Ceantt, Connolly, and Plunkett) were court-martialed and shot in Kilmainham Jail within a few weeks. O'Rahilly had died in the fighting, and, after a more standard trial, Casement was hanged in an English prison in early August. The only local commander to escape death was Eamon de Valera, a mathematics teacher recruited into the Irish Volunteers. Instead, like Michael Collins, he was sent to prison in England.

It might be said the British miscalculated twice. The theory of General Sir John Maxwell, who had served in Egypt and looked forward to returning there once he had put down the rebellion, was that a definitive, brutal military response was the best way to end any talk of treason. It's how he would treat fanatical Muslims, and he shared the English conviction that the Irish, like the Arabs or the Turks, were an inferior race in need of a strong hand. Also, the Irish rebels, who were complete amateurs in military matters, had embarrassed the English officers who thought to lead a classic cavalry charge across the bridges and through the narrow streets of Dublin. Brightly clad lancers and their mounts had been gunned down from windows and rooftops. There were many unexpected English widows and orphans who deserved a severe reckoning for their grief, and Maxwell meant to provide it for them.

The first mistake was in thinking that by eliminating the ringleaders, even dumping their bodies in quicklime so as to forestall the funeral rites that might become an occasion for untoward public displays, the ordinary Dubliner would be so intimidated that good British order could prevail unchallenged. The Irish responded in a quite opposite manner. The rebels, who had been jeered by their fellow citizens upon their surrender, now gained the status of political saints. Pearse, who had electrified his audience at the funeral of an old Fenian leader by declaiming that "While Ireland holds these graves, Ireland unfree shall never be at peace," joined the elite pantheon of martyrs for independence.

Arguably the second mistake was too quick an effort to achieve a greater sense of normalcy by releasing the prisoners—many of them by Christmas and the rest the following year—and allowing them to resume their organizing. De Valera, spared the firing squad in part because of his American citizenship, was counted as a hero of the uprising. His defiant conduct in prison had solidified his reputation among the other men jailed for their participation in the rebellion. He returned to effectively displace Arthur Griffith as the head of Sinn Fein, the group which had undeservedly come to be so linked with the uprising that at the time all rebels were referred to as Sinn Feiners.

Michael Collins, who was a close friend of Sean McDermott, had been equally unrepentant in prison. His own tactics, which set a standard that would be followed through the rest of this century, were to make life as difficult as possible for his English jailors. At his urging Irishmen refused to identify themselves, demanded prisoner of war status, and undertook a hunger strike to protest being treated as ordinary criminals. Their actions generated immense public sympathy, and the British decided on amnesty as the lesser evil. Even more than de Valera, it was Collins who guaranteed that Dublin had been only an opening skirmish in the war for independence.

What the British government needed was men for the trenches of Europe—men who might yet be drafted in Ireland and men who would come from America if the United States could be persuaded to enter the war. Amnesty for the rebels was meant to lessen the opposition to the war effort in both Ireland and the United States, where the Irish emigrants were proving to be a powerful political force. What it did, however, was return militants such as de Valera and Collins to take advantage of the British decision to go ahead with conscripting Irish men to fight and die on the Continent at a time when the idea of wearing a uniform and playing soldier had lost its appeal.

Even if the Irish could forget how British troopers had blasted their way through Dublin, the cheerful bravado of 1914 had long since been dissolved in the sheer horror of seemingly endless trench warfare in which death came from a yellow gas as readily as from a spray of machine gun bullets. Even the idea that future independence might be the reward for continued loyalty was clouded by the talk of partition. Afraid to antagonize the Protestants of Ulster and so lose their support—or worse, precipitate the Protestant rebellion that had been brewing even before the opening shots of the First World War—Lloyd George's government had accepted the proposal to exempt the six northeast counties, where Protestants held a numerical majority, from any home rule legislation. According to Lloyd

George, this was to be the case no matter how any vote for independence turned out in Ulster itself.

In early April 1918, almost two years after the Easter Rebellion, the British government, still debating some form of home rule for Ireland, passed the Military Service Bill. In Ireland the reaction was immediate and powerful, and in Dublin, Irish officials adopted de Valera's language that the act authorizing conscription "must be regarded as a declaration of war on the Irish nation." The Catholic bishops stated that this was "an oppressive and inhuman law which the Irish people have a right to resist by every means that are consonant with the law of God." The British government responded the next month by rounding up the most prominent of the Irish activists on a charge of cooperating with the Germans. De Valera was back in jail and Collins began his "life on the bicycle" as a wanted man who had support even from some of the Irish police who were supposed to track him down.

England's war on the Continent ended a few months later, but its war on its neighboring island was just beginning.

The Easter Rebellion had been a violent act carried out by men who took no delight in violence and in fact attempted to play by rules of war that their enemy too easily ignored. The rebels were also men who were resigned to death when they took their stand in Dublin, and in part they knew they were bound to fail because their fear of informants had kept them from any really serious degree of organization and coordination. They had hoped to surprise both the English and their fellow Irish, but the best they could hope for was that massive public support would put the British troops in a state of siege in their own barracks. They knew soon enough that they had overestimated the Dubliners and underestimated the English. Still, they took pride in the fact that their own men, compelled to a degree of abstinence that was meant to go against the stereotype of the drunken Irishman, had behaved as honorable soldiers, treating their prisoners as well as civilians decently even though they justifiably expected not to be treated at all as well themselves.

Michael Collins, who had made a study of the tactics of the Boer rebels in South Africa, was a completely different kind of adversary. He was an utterly ruthless guerrilla who saw no particular advantage in standing up to be shot. Instead, he completely turned around the British system of informants by developing a far more efficient spy system of his own, worked seriously on arming his men in any way he could, and established that his new army would be composed of snipers and bombers who would never make the Easter rebels' mistake of attempting to take a building and hold it. Among the actions that would characterize this new Irish Republican Army, as the volunteers came to be called in 1919, were assassinations and jail breaks; both had the effect of undermining any belief in the British ability to maintain the normal conventions of a criminal justice system. Law and order went together, after all, and with the breakdown of both the British would be forced to withdraw—or so it was believed.

The first twentieth-century proclamation of an Irish Republic had been in April 1916. The second was just three years later, again in April. Members of Sinn Fein met in Dublin for the First Dail and elected de Valera president. The Irish constabulary were defined as agents of the British government to be shunned by the people as spies, traitors, and perjurers. Members of the "G" squad (the original G-men, even before American mobsters began using the term), which was supposed to deal with subversion, were given fair warning that they could be targeted for death.

For a while the new rebels hoped that the talks at Versailles, aimed at reshaping European politics, would include support for full independence. Home rule—even the type of dual monarchy originally professed by Sinn Fein's founder—was no longer an option. American support was considered crucial, and the Sinn Fein tradition of hosting Irish-American delegations come on fact-finding missions began when an American trio, which included the former mayor of Chicago and governor of Illinois, was given a rapid tour of the country. What mattered at the end, however, was that President Wilson was not about to break with Lloyd George over Ireland; he was more concerned with pulling everyone together in order to create the League of Nations.

Michael Collins began making good on the threat to kill British policemen. He formed a special team of assassins, a dozen committed young men who meant to save Ireland from English spies—and the Dail had already pronounced that the members of the Royal Irish Constabulary should be seen as spies. The first to die was a detective named Smith. The British reacted by declaring Sinn Fein an illegal organization and raiding its Dublin headquarters. Collins's response was to have another detective killed.

In describing these events in his biography of Michael Collins, Tim Pat Coogan emphasizes the moral atmosphere in which the hit men worked by pointing out how one of them, going to confession and admitting to killing a man, was asked whether he had believed he was doing the right thing. When he replied that he had had no qualms about his action, the priest told him to carry on the good work and gave him absolution. In their own minds these IRA men were soldiers carrying out legitimate acts of war. What would have been wrong, as Collins told one of them, was to kill for strictly personal reasons, such as a desire for revenge. The volunteer was to kill only when under orders to do so.

Collins was one of those who had to give such orders, and according to Coogan, he did so because he had come to believe that his war for independence could be won in no other way. He was not an enthusiastic killer, however. Other leaders of the IRA, such as Cathal Brugha, were even less so, and one of the internal debates, won by Collins, was over whether ambushing and killing their targets without warning was justifiable. According to Coogan, Brugha was concerned about eventually having to answer to an international tribunal for war crimes and so had wanted to document each "execution" very carefully.

Inevitably the police, now being gunned down with impunity, would have to be replaced with far more heavily armed men having no compunction about following a shoot-to-kill policy. This was exactly what Collins wanted. The description of the British justice system as essentially the apparatus of an occupying force led to a set of reactions that in fact confirmed the description. It was a no-win situation for the English, but it was to take two years of bloodshed before they came to see that they had played right into the hands of their enemy.

De Valera may have been the announced president of the Irish Republic—which at this point had no greater standing than it had three years before, when Pearse and his colleagues announced it in the broadsides circulated in Dublin—but Collins was the man who controlled the course of events. His use of assassination, combined with the hit-and-run tactics of his so-called flying columns, brought exactly the type of English retaliation guaranteed to unite the Irish people—at least the Catholics—behind Sinn Fein.

There was nothing subtle about the manner in which British authorities actively recruited Irish Protestants, many of them unemployed veterans of the First World War, who had long been spoiling for a chance to put the Catholics in their place. Nor was there any particular subtlety in the recruiting of ex-servicemen in England who were willing to cross the channel to make Ireland "a hell for rebels." The mercenaries, seen as adjuncts to the police rather than as proper soldiers, were outfitted in a mix of military khaki and constabulary black (leading the Irish to label them as "black and tans," after a breed of hunting dog). They were supposedly to be kept in

line by the Police Auxiliary Cadets, recruited from former British officers and now outfitted in dashing blue uniforms with a gun on each
hip. The Tans and the Auxis immediately made their presence felt in
Irish cities by shooting them up, and the IRA, now with the complete
support of the people, began shooting back.

Mutual murder quickly became the norm, not just in the streets
and fields where Irish guerrillas shot it out with the British security
forces, but also inside private homes where assassins on both sides
took out their targets. Anyone with known republican sympathies
could expect to die as had Thomas MacCurtain, lord mayor of Cork,
shot dead in front of his wife by a group of men with blackened faces
who had forced their way into his house. British informants, especially those who had taken on the risky business of being double
agents, could expect to die as did the nineteen men killed in the early
hours of Ireland's first "Bloody Sunday" (November 21, 1920). Ordinary people who would never have thought to take up the gun themselves could expect to die in reprisal shootings, as did the fourteen
players and spectators massacred on a Dublin football field that
same afternoon.

If there was a difference between the sides, it was this: the volunteers killed selectively and often worried about the rightness of what
they had done or were about to do; the British killed with far more
gusto and often, as in the incident at the football field, with virtually
no regard for the lives of noncombatants. One reason for this difference was that the volunteers were well known in their communities,
and since most were very young men with a rigid Catholic upbringing, there were social limits on their behavior that did not exist
among the Black and Tans or the Auxiliaries, who were far from
home and had implicit carte blanche to use any level of violence
they wanted.

Compounding the potential for excessive force was the creation in
the north of the B Specials, typically former Ulster Volunteers, described by David Fitzpatrick as "a private army with police badges,"
who saw their mission as keeping the Catholic minority in line. Their
leader was Colonel William Bliss Spender, the man who had helped
arm the original Ulster Volunteers with guns illegally brought in
along the Antrim coast in 1914. The British government clearly was
not opposed to paramilitary groups in Ireland, provided they were
proper Protestants who could be counted on to accept the equation
(still so apparent in the rhetoric of the north) of republicanism and
Catholicism.

The IRA did manage to take the war to England itself. This was nothing new, since the IRB had set off bombs during the Fenian uprising of 1867. Liverpool was particularly hard hit, and British intelligence became aware that the IRA had been planning to destroy Liverpool's shipping and Manchester's electricity in April 1921. It could have been worse: Cathal Brugha, nominally Collins's boss in military matters because he was the rebel government's defense minister, had talked of hits against Cabinet ministers and using submachine guns on citizens lining up for the movies, but Collins refused to go along with such tactics.

In addition to the military aspects of its campaign, the IRA managed to draw world attention to the Irish cause with another time-honored tactic—the hunger strike. MacCurtain's successor as lord mayor of Cork was Terence MacSwiney, arrested in August 1921. MacSwiney and ten other men arrested with him refused to eat until they were released. In October, MacSwiney and Joseph Murphy, one of the others arrested, were dead, and the others broke their fast only at the urging of Arthur Griffith. Since MacSwiney had been transferred to England, the citizens of London were able to watch uniformed volunteers form an honor guard to accompany his body through the streets. Despite Lloyd George's efforts to minimize the political significance of the funeral, the people of Ireland stopped work for a national day of mourning on the day of his burial in Cork.

There had been serious talk of peace since the beginning of 1921. At Christmas the military had come to Westminster to argue against a cease-fire on the basis that they were winning the war, and that if martial law could be declared throughout Ireland, by summer ninety percent of the people would be on the British side. On the other hand, a cease-fire would only give Sinn Fein time to consolidate its hold, and open elections were an impossibility because Collins would keep the people from voting. Lloyd George, as Coogan points out, did note the inconsistency in what was being reported by the generals: How could the military solution be counted a success if Collins continued to exert such influence?

What did happen was that there were elections in May. By the end of summer a peace treaty between England and Ireland was being negotiated.

Collins, who had repeatedly escaped capture while managing a number of daring actions against British authorities, by now had an almost mythic stature with the enemy. His standing with those who should have been friends and allies was hardly that secure. Brugha hated him, and de Valera, who had only limited success in winning over American politicians when he was shipped over to the United States in 1919, deeply resented him. There was a clear difference in personalities that carried over into their concepts of policy. Brugha and de Valera were ideal bureaucrats, obsessed by the need to have exact records and strict accounts. Collins, the handsome and charming "Big Fellow," was the charismatic leader who seemed blessed by the gods with incredible luck. Brugha and de Valera preferred to think in terms of open warfare regardless of the risk to the volunteers. Collins carried on operations that were intended to neutralize his enemy with minimal risk to his own men. De Valera did get his way in an attack that destroyed the Custom House in Dublin, but he lost more than eighty men to death, injury, or capture. This was clearly unacceptable, since the total number of volunteers in all brigades was never more than a few thousand, whereas the combined British forces were in the tens of thousands.

The attack on the Custom House was on May 25. The day before, there had been an election that in effect established partition, with voting taking place for both a northern and a southern parliament. Sinn Fein, which in a general election in 1918 had won a majority in every county but the most strongly Protestant (Antrim, Derry, Armagh, and Down), worked together with the Nationalist party and made even a better showing.

The public relations effect of the Custom House attack pushed the British to work harder to achieve a peace, one way or another. On May 26, Westminster called for martial law if the southern parliament was not functioning by July 12. The day before this deadline, there was a truce that, backing away from earlier British preconditions, allowed the IRA to keep its weapons. The actual negotiations of a peace went slowly. De Valera wanted complete independence for all of the island, but Lloyd George was willing to grant only a very limited amount of self-government that excluded the six mainly Protestant counties of the north. In the final act of this drama, Collins, against his own inclinations, was part of the delegation that achieved a treaty in December.

It was not a treaty that de Valera found acceptable. There was now to be a twenty-six-county Irish Free State with a parliament that swore loyalty to the Crown. It barely won acceptance in the Dail, and de Valera walked away from his office as president. Collins became the man who now exercised power in the transition from a British province to a separate country. He also had to deal with rebellion, particularly in Limerick. In April 1922 there was full-scale civil war with the IRA fighting against those who supported the treaty, and in August, Collins was killed in an ambush in County Cork.

In the next few years de Valera returned to power, cutting himself off from the old Sinn Fein in 1926 to form Fianna Fail, long to be the Republic's dominant political party. Now it was his turn to fight his former colleagues, the unrepentant IRA men who would not accommodate themselves to a divided country. Ironically, more rebels were executed by de Valera than by the British in 1916.

The official position of the Irish Republican Army from de Valera's time to the present is that the only legitimate government of Ireland is the IRA itself, with authority derived from the Dail of 1918. First Collins and then de Valera had failed to bring about what those who called themselves republicans insisted on: a single government for all thirty-two counties. Despite the wording of the Irish Constitution, which claims sovereignty over the six northern counties, the Free State—which became the Republic of Ireland in 1949, a year after Fianna Fail had fallen from power—did not attempt forcible reunion. The IRA itself was outlawed in 1936, and in 1939 de Valera had its members declared traitors to the Irish state.

The parallels between the situation three-quarters of a century ago and the present are striking. Granted, it is Belfast and Derry rather than Dublin and Cork that are the cities most affected, but the rhetoric from all three sides—republican, unionist, and British—remains much the same. Even today's debate over "decommissioning" weapons as a precondition of negotiations echoes what was being said in 1920. The hunger strikes of the postwar period were repeated in 1981, and obviously the explosions in London and Manchester repeat the events of 1921. Whatever the mutations over the decades, the IRA sees itself continuing the grand tradition of the Easter Rebellion just as the various groups on the Protestant side trace their lineage to the original Ulster Volunteers and members of the British security apparatus repeat the mistakes of their own predecessors in the Black and Tan War.

As an American I find this somewhat bewildering. In my own country there can be changes of outlook that occur so quickly that even the recent past seems like a different world. The antagonism toward Germany and Japan of the 1940s was completely reversed during the Cold War that set the United States against its former ally, the Soviet Union. The South torn apart by the battle over integration in the 1960s a generation later provides models of racial harmony.

The same rapidity of change characterizes other parts of the world as well, sometimes positively and other times far less so. The Soviet

Union has already been dissolved, and Russians are learning to be good capitalists who have to worry about a crime rate out of control. The austere China of the earlier People's Republic has given way to a new era of hedonism and self-advancement. Cities once cited as models of ethnic cooperation—Beirut and Sarajevo, in particular— now evidence how bad things can be when old hatreds resurface, yet Cairo and Jerusalem stand as testimony to what is possible when old hatreds can be set aside.

Nowhere, however, does continuity reign so strongly as it does in Ireland. To understand the present, it is more important here than anywhere else to understand the past, and this is largely because much of the ceremonial life of the country, both Catholic and Protestant, is a constant invocation of the past. In part this can be traced to the heritage of both Catholics, whose version of their faith is far more conservative than that of their European coreligionists, and Protestants, who have tended to see earthly life in the dour terms of Scottish Calvinism.

Another factor is Ireland's relatively slow-changing economy. A third is the simple fact that Ireland is an island, and physical insularity does appear to have a strong psychological dimension. Yet a fourth, perhaps too little appreciated, is that any people denied an official history—as were the Catholics of Ireland during the Protestant Ascendancy—will attach greater importance to an unofficial one. Past rebellions that failed provide the impetus for new ones that might succeed, and even the most violent tactics associated with dead heroes of the past are justified by that association.

Michael Collins, "the man who made Ireland," as Tim Pat Coogan labels him, was one of those rare individuals who was able to think in terms transcending his own past and present. He learned from South Africa how to fight the British in a new way, and with a combination of uncanny luck and shrewd planning, he managed to defeat some of the most capable military and political figures of his time. Coogan argues that because of Collins's pragmatism and his economic vision, Ireland would have benefited immensely had he lived. Yet, ironic as it was that his charmed life was ended by an IRA man's bullet, it was also an indication of the problem that every talented Irish leader must face: the more he moves toward the future, the more he risks losing the support of those who still look to the past. The ultimate tragedy would be that Collins is remembered more for his death squads than for his vision of a new Ireland.

When I was first in Belfast, I was told that there had been a piece of graffiti that invited Gerry Adams to remember what had happened to Michael Collins. I do not know whether it was a Catholic or a Protestant who wrote it, but clearly it was a warning, and it was a warning that made sense coming from either side. If Adams wanted to be the diplomat who did not dissociate himself clearly from the IRA, he faced death from extremists on the Protestant side. If he wanted to be the diplomat who made too many concessions for the sake of peace, he faced death from extremists within the IRA itself. And then, of course, there were those who might see his death as a vehicle to further destabilize the situation in Northern Ireland to the advantage of all those British operatives who have seen themselves charged with the task of ending insurrection by any means necessary.

6

The Troubles

Commitment to the Republican Movement is the firm belief that
its struggle both military and political is morally justified, that war
is morally justified and that the Army is the direct representatives
[sic] of the 1918 Dail Eirann Parliament, and that as such they are
the legal and lawful government of the Irish Republic.

The IRA Training Manual (*Green Book*), cited by
Brendan O'Brien in *The Long War:*
The IRA and Sinn Fein 1985 to Today

Various writers have attempted to explain the IRA in terms of the
strict Catholic upbringing of most of its members. This can obviously
be overdone—for instance, volunteers are not motivated by a desire
for martyrdom, nor is there any notion of a Catholic *jihad* against a
non-Catholic enemy—but what does appear true enough is that
there is a constant concern with moral justification that seldom appears in either British or American discussions of policy.

The *Green Book* of the 1970s begins with a discussion of commitment to the republican movement that insists on the moral legitimacy of its violence. This runs parallel to the "just war" concept of
Catholic moral theology, which would not easily condone rebellion
against a legitimate government but would allow force to free a
country from an illegitimate one. What becomes especially important, then, is that the volunteer see himself as part of the only legiti-

mate Irish government—the one established in 1918. The government of the Free State, according to this view, is as much a usurper as the British provincial administration in Northern Ireland.

Here the natural Irish tendency to root a present practice in tradition (a tendency common to all the peoples of the British Isles) might be said to merge with the Catholic notion of an apostolic succession. Even the humblest priest celebrating Mass outdoors on a rock was linked with the church of St. Peter in a way that no Presbyterian minister could claim. The IRA man might be a relatively uneducated laborer, but he was linked to the men who brought about the Easter Rebellion and then established a government of their own in 1918.

The obvious question for the outsider is why the government of the Free State that emerged from the treaty of 1921 was not legitimate. The republican answer, like an article of faith that is not meant to be particularly logical, is that those who signed the treaty—Collins and Griffith and the others, even though all used the Irish rather than the English versions of their names—had accepted partition, and by this heresy they had waived the right to represent the one true faith of Irish politics.

Given the effort to retain a linkage with the original Easter rebels, it is understandable why the notion of socialism, which was less compatible with a Catholic outlook, remained part of the republican belief system. James Connolly, the labor leader who was shot while strapped to a chair in the Kilmainham jail because he could not stand on his gangrenous leg, had been a strong advocate of socialism, even to the point of predicting on ideological grounds that British capitalists would not allow the shelling of Dublin. The *Green Book* continues this by insisting that the long-term objective of the IRA is the "Establishment of a Democratic Socialist Republic." Accordingly, the *gardai* and the Free State army (republicans still are reluctant to speak of the present Irish government in terms of a republic but insist on the old designation of the Free State) are lumped together with the police and military of the north as having tasks that are "treasonable and as such morally wrong, politically unacceptable and ethically inexcusable."

De Valera's efforts to eradicate the IRA in the south were fairly successful. There was no longer popular support for IRA actions against his government, and the only areas in which republican feelings ran high were the British-controlled counties and the other counties of Ireland that were on the border (especially Donegal, Monaghan, and Louth). The IRA did again set off bombs in England in 1939, but its attempted association with Nazi Germany only inten-sified both British and Irish efforts to counter what remaining influ-ence the group possessed.

The bombing campaign also cost the IRA the allegiance of Sean MacBride, son of Major John MacBride and the actress Maud Gonne. The senior MacBride had been one of those shot in the weeks after the Easter Rebellion, and his son had attempted to carry on the revo-lutionary tradition of his parents. He had been the IRA chief of staff between 1936 and 1938, and he remained active in support of those interned by the British. He was one of the founders of Amnesty Inter-national, was awarded the Nobel Peace Prize in 1974, and is perhaps best known for the MacBride Principles, which are aimed at over-coming discrimination through economic sanctions.

After the war, during which de Valera's Ireland had joined Spain and Switzerland in remaining neutral, the IRA did not really again go on the offensive until the border campaign of 1956–62. Many Volun-teers had sat out the war interned in the Curragh, a bleak detention camp in County Kildare. Sean MacBride, who had the advantage of having been an IRA leader himself, led the legal campaign that led to the freedom of fifty-three men. Those who remained lived a dismal existence, studying the Irish language (something that would be-come a tradition among republican prisoners) and debating ideol-ogy in the face of the all too obvious fact that they had been marginalized in the Ireland they sought to unite.

According to J. Bowyer Bell (in an essay reprinted in *The Gun in Politics: An Analysis of Irish Political Conflict, 1916–1986*), the deci-sion to return to violence was made in 1951, and during the next five years the IRA rebuilt itself, raiding British barracks in both England and the north for its weapons and gradually adding to its corps of volunteers. The campaign began in late 1956, was met by stiff reac-tion in both the north and the south, and by 1962 had reached its end as the Army Council ordered a stand-down. The IRA seemed moribund, increasingly irrelevant in a divided Ireland that was mov-ing forward economically.

What changed everything was the Irish adaptation of the civil rights protests of the United States. Discrimination against Catholics was part of the reality of the north, and new figures were emerging who decided to make use of the tactics of American black leaders. In cities such as Derry and Belfast there were demonstrations that pro-voked reaction from Catholic-baiting young toughs. Bernadette Devlin, advanced as a compromise candidate in a 1969 election in mid-Ulster, made the international headlines as one of the new

Catholic militants. Sinn Fein had consistently followed an abstentionist policy according to which its candidates might win elections
to the British Parliament but would refuse to take their seats. Now,
with Sinn Fein backing, the brash young woman did go to London,
where she was going to be heard one way or another.

The situation worsened in the north with firebombings that forced
Catholics living in Protestant areas to leave their homes and take
refuge in enclaves such as the Falls in Belfast and the Bogside in
Derry. To keep order, London sent in the troops, who were initially
welcomed by the besieged Catholics. Tragically, like the Royal Ulster
Constabulary, most of the soldiers identified with the Protestants
rather than the Catholics, and in a short time anyone in any type of
British uniform came to be seen as an enemy. Rioting was now a
daily activity, and parts of Derry and Belfast became no-go zones
controlled by the IRA. On January 30, 1972, Ireland experienced another "Bloody Sunday" when paratroopers opened fire on unarmed
civilians in Derry, killing fourteen. Violent response from the IRA,
which resulted in the killing of still more civilians, only outraged
world opinion, and in late May the Army Council of the "Official" IRA
declared an indefinite cease-fire.

By this time there was no longer just one IRA. For a number of
years there had been increasing tension between those willing to
work toward a unified Ireland through more standard political
means and those who wanted to take on the British in all-out warfare. The seeming ineffectiveness of the "Official" IRA, now headed
by Cathal Goulding, led to the appearance in 1968 of a breakaway
group, the "Provisional" IRA with Sean MacStiofan (born John
Stevenson) as its chief of staff. The Officials ("Stickies") and the Provos were not about to coexist easily, especially in the rough streets of
West Belfast, and volunteers were as likely to spend their time plot-
ting how to kill each other as planning new operations against the
British. All this was happening while various groups on the Protestant side set out to kill anyone from the IRA and typically settled for
anyone who was Catholic.

Two of the younger men caught up in the violent scene were Martin McGuinness in Derry and Gerry Adams in Belfast. McGuinness,
originally an Official who went over to the Provos, allegedly orches-
trated the car bombings that leveled much of what British interests
owned in Derry. Adams, who came from a family in which imprisonment for republican activities had become a male vocation, moved
quickly to become a principal Sinn Fein spokesman. Ironically, it had
been support for what is called "constitutionalism"—a willingness to

accept the legitimacy of the Constitution voted on in 1922—that had led to the break. Now it was the Provos who saw the significance of actively participating in the electoral process, even if they would still be "abstentionists" who would refuse to be seated if elected.

In 1981 IRA man Bobby Sands, fasting to death in a British prison camp outside of Belfast, was elected to Parliament. The fact that Prime Minister Margaret Thatcher refused any concessions to Sands or the other hunger strikers drew world attention, and Sands's death effectively put the IRA, which had now taken over Sinn Fein, back in the running as a political force that had to be dealt with. In 1982 Adams easily won a seat in what was to be a new Assembly for Northern Ireland.

One striking photo from that period, used for the jacket of the American edition of Tim Pat Coogan's 1996 book, *The Troubles*, is of the funeral procession for Bobby Sands in Belfast. It was taken by an American photographer, John McGonigle. I met McGonigle shortly after the book appeared, and I heard something more of the story behind the picture. Adams is prominent as one of the pallbearers, and British security was determined to neutralize the importance of the funeral. Videocameras mounted on the armored vehicles used by security forces allowed the British to identify all those photographing the event, and a systematic effort was made to get hold of their film. John managed to get away with what he believed to be the only known picture of the scene, but he also took a photo of a determined trooper who, as he told me, was fully prepared to kill him. From then on, he was carefully watched every time he landed at Heathrow on a flight from the United States, and he still felt that his life was in jeopardy.

In Northern Ireland both the IRA and the British security forces understood the importance of controlling information. Television cameras had changed the course of political life in the United States. With that in mind, the IRA made full use of the fact that continued rioting drew news coverage and created a worldwide image of Belfast as a dangerous city despite the fact that for most of its citizens it was a far safer place to live than Washington or New York or Los Angeles. The British, for the same reason, worked hard to limit access to anything that might show their security forces in a bad light. The IRA wanted the world to see the Brits as a brutal occupying army. The British in turn wanted to maintain an image of the IRA as a group of extremists terrorizing the Catholics of areas such as the Falls and the Bogside. Sands's funeral was a wonderful photo op in that it was a classic instance of the republican apotheosis of the fallen volunteer, and for just that reason British security acted more harshly.

A portrait of Bobby Sands covers the side of the building housing the Sinn Fein offices on Lower Falls Road in Belfast. It is, I think, the largest of the political wall murals that are part of the popular culture in that divided city, and in their deaths Sands and seven other prisoners succeeded in mobilizing world opinion on the republican side. After the Easter Rebellion there had been hunger strikes in an effort to force the British to recognize volunteers as prisoners of war rather than as ordinary criminals. In the early 1970s, as the British adopted widespread internment of supposed "terrorists" in places such as the newly built Maze ten miles outside Belfast, but again denied them any special status, a number of volunteers refused to wear prison-issued clothing and instead went "on the blanket." Finally denied elementary sanitary facilities, they had to live with their own waste in what came to be called the Dirty Protest. Hunger strikes were the last and most desperate option, and just as before, men did fast to the death.

The IRA, either the waning Officials or the new and more militant Provisionals, was not the only republican group represented in the Maze. In 1974 a number of former Officials, with Seamus Costello leading them, established the Irish Republican Socialist Party together with the Irish National Liberation Army. The INLA saw itself as explicitly "Trotskyite" and identified strongly with parallel revolutionary movements in other countries. Its tactics would be just as violent as those of the IRA, and it was responsible for one of the more dramatic assassinations, the killing of Margaret Thatcher's close associate Airy Neave in 1979. The IRA's own best-known hit took place the year before, when Lord Mountbatten was blown up on his yacht in County Sligo.

The incessant, attention-getting shootings and bombings were designed to keep the ordinary English citizen well aware that the war was not just being fought across the Irish Sea. The strategy was not much different from the one followed by Michael Collins. Neither was the logic behind it. The ultimate justification for killing anyone Irish connected with the British police or military was that such a person was a traitor (assuming, obviously, that the IRA was to be seen as the only legitimate government for all of Ireland), and the ultimate justification for striking at English officials, even the ambassador to Ireland (Christopher Ewart-Biggs, killed by a road mine outside of Dublin in 1976), was that they were the enemy.

In one way the INLA had an easier task in rationalizing its violence. Costello, caught up in a Marxist ideology, could always echo Lenin that in a capitalist world the only morality was that which forwarded the revolution; only afterward, with class divisions destroyed, could there be a genuine moral outlook that respected all human beings equally. The IRA required the more tortured reasoning that appears in the *Green Book*, by which the volunteer first identified his own group as the sole legitimate authority in Ireland and then applied the concept of the just war.

To those affected by IRA and INLA actions, the ordinary citizens in England in particular, the theology of paramilitary violence was too arcane to be understood easily. Instead, the operative word, always used by the authorities and repeated in the media, was "terrorism," with its implication of completely amoral actions that were no more than extortion on a grander scale. The British, who took pride in the fact they had not submitted to Nazi Germany despite destruction far worse than anything within the reach of the Irish, readily supported the emergency powers by which anything resembling a normal criminal justice system disappeared in Northern Ireland.

During the Anglo-Irish War, the British had never felt that they had a free hand to apply all their military might. Instead, they attempted to retain the semblance of police actions by their use of the Tans and the Auxis, who nonetheless managed to act like an invading army. In this new war in the north, the military were brought in to provide a level of response beyond that of the RUC, but now the problem was that search-and-destroy missions in Catholic areas of the major cities would inevitably bring about even a greater level of destruction than that accomplished by the rampaging Protestant mobs during the civil rights protests, and so risked intervention from the Republic. Realistically, the troopers had to concede whole neighborhoods to their enemy. Their one hope was that they could interdict the transport of men and weapons along the lightly traveled roads of the Irish countryside.

The architect of security in Northern Ireland was Brigadier Frank Kitson, assigned to the north in 1970 after establishing himself as an expert on counterinsurgency in other parts of the British Empire. History did not quite repeat itself, since Kitson was not another General Sir John Maxwell determined to kill off the rebels. As discussed by journalists Patrick Bishop and Eamonn Mallie in their history, *The Provisional IRA*, Kitson thought the mission was "to wean the Catholic population away from the terrorists" through what he identified as deescalation and attrition. The first would involve community action projects to remedy Catholic grievances. The second would be widespread arrests of suspected terrorists. It is no surprise that only his second idea is remembered.

If Kitson had been given his way, all adult male Catholics would have been subjected to a few days of detention in which there would be intensive interrogation under conditions certain to break down their resistance. As it happened, the security forces were allowed to bring in anyone whom they even remotely suspected of terrorism and use pain-inducing techniques that Amnesty International would condemn as torture, although one British statement was that they should not be thought of as torture because inflicting pain was not something that gave pleasure to the interrogators.

At the same time the British armed forces, which had some of the best fighting men in the world in its Special Air Services, went on the offensive against the IRA in the field. According to one of the men caught up in the action, Paul Bruce, this was a covert war that included executions and then random shootings in the Falls area of Belfast. I had found his newly released book, *The Nemesis File: The True Story of an SAS Execution Squad*, prominently displayed in London bookstores on my second trip to Britain early in 1996, and it was a horrifying example of what various writers, including thriller writer Victor O'Reilly in *Rules of the Hunt*, have termed "big boys' rules." Essentially it is the idea that "terrorists" are fair game to be hunted and killed without any of the niceties of a legal hearing.

The question of whether there really was any policy by which supposed terrorists would be shot on sight did come up dramatically after a couple of incidents in late 1982, just outside Lurgan in County Armagh. In an effort to uncover the truth about what had happened, a Manchester police official named John Stalker was dispatched to Northern Ireland. Stalker soon discovered that the RUC was "stonewalling" the investigation; then he was pulled off the case and suddenly charged with improprieties in his own conduct back in England. Eventually he was vindicated, but what came to be called the Stalker Affair was clear evidence of a blatant disregard for the rule of law on the part of those charged with enforcing it. It did seem that Irishmen could be gunned down with impunity by members of the security forces. Hearings, either before or after the fact, were not needed.

The legal hearings themselves had undergone a drastic change at the recommendation of Lord Diplock in 1972. As Bishop and Mallie sum it up, suspects could be arrested on a soldier's word, juries were abolished, confessions (often gained through the intense and prolonged interrogation allowed under special legislation) were allowed to stand unless torture could be proven in court, and where the possession of weapons was involved, the burden of proof shifted from prosecutor to defendant. Key principles of Anglo-American law were thus thrown overboard.

The IRA itself adapted to changing conditions. Later versions of the *Green Book* reflected the move away from the brigade organization developed a half-century earlier to a structure better able to resist efforts at infiltration. In theory, volunteers now operated in small groups (cells), with no man knowing more about others in the IRA than he needed to. Moreover, they were to tell no one of their membership—not their family, not their sweethearts. Membership was pared to the hundreds, perhaps a tenth of what it had been when the so-called Troubles were well under way in the early 1970s. Now the emphasis was on commitment, even if this was for a fairly short period. The true volunteer in an active service unit could be a bank robber, if that is what was needed to gain funds, or a shooter willing to "kneecap" (shoot through the knees) a petty criminal from the neighborhood, or a sniper willing to gun down an RUC officer, or a bomber ready to deliver his package to a designated target. He might get paid a basic stipend, typically what could be made by going on the dole, and if he were imprisoned, he might expect his family to be looked after. If he were killed, he would be remembered in annual commemorations along with all those who had died on active service from the Easter Rebellion onward.

To what extent was the IRA a Catholic army waging war against Protestants? One thing that is striking about the republican rhetoric, which is expressed nowhere more strongly than in the early *Green Book*, is the manner in which it downplays religion. In part this may be due to the Marxian orientation dominating the IRA before the split between Officials and Provisionals: all religious institutions are seen as repressive, and given the historical antagonism between most of the Irish hierarchy and the rebels, it would be unlikely that a volunteer is encouraged to see himself defending his church. Loyalists have been targets for IRA action not because they are anti-Catholic (which so many are) but because they are pro-British.

The most complex aspect of the story of the northern counties is the way in which sectarian conflict has such a clearly religious dimension with Protestants, especially the rampaging Orangemen who threaten Catholic neighborhoods each summer as marching season begins, and such a clearly political dimension with the Catholics. Volunteers have at times retaliated for the killing of Catholics by a random killing of Protestants, but these have been exceptions. The random killing of Catholics, on the other hand, was a characteristic feature of loyalist murder gangs such as Lenny Murphy's Shankill Butchers (the basis for Eoin McNamee's chilling 1994 novel, *Resurrection Man*).

While preparing this chapter, I thought of the difference between a city such as Belfast during the Troubles and my own Los Angeles. In the black and brown neighborhoods of my city there are far more teenage gangsters than there are policemen, and as likely as not, the teenagers are better armed with automatic weapons. In Belfast, where RUC stations are ugly barricaded buildings, a relative handful of IRA men on one side or overly zealous Orangemen on the other can make life hell for their enemy, yet with all the resources of the United Kingdom they are grossly outnumbered, and in terms of weaponry are totally overmatched. A key difference, one that has existed since the war with England three-quarters of a century ago, is that the IRA is a true guerrilla force with a high degree of support within the community. The same can be said of the leading Protestant paramilitary organizations.

In Los Angeles, a teenage gangster goes through the revolving door of the criminal justice system, and his community wonders why he cannot be off the streets longer. In Belfast, the innocent might be as likely to be interned, but no prisoner is ever quite seen as deserving his punishment—at least not by members of his own community. Oddly, I have tended to feel safer in Belfast, if for no other reason than that I was less likely to be caught up in a purely random shooting.

Another difference is that any proposed solution to gang violence in Los Angeles—whether through social reforms or through police and court action—arguably requires expenditures of money and manpower that Americans find intolerable. One result is that victims and perpetrators make the newspapers or the evening news only when death is dealt out in a particularly outrageous manner. In the northern counties, with a total population about a quarter of the metropolitan area of Los Angeles, violence can still be understood in terms of specific persons. Individual incidents can be recorded and dissected, and—something I would find unimaginable in my own city—a writer named Malcolm Sutton can produce a book that indexes all thirty-three hundred people killed in the Troubles from 1969 to 1993. There is at least the illusion of intelligibility.

But this may be no more than an illusion. Many writers would like to believe it is possible to reduce the conflicts of the north to a manageable set of factors so that, like some strictly technical problem in social engineering, a clear program for peace emerges. Certainly the lectures comprising much of the early *Green Book* reflect such a belief. The harsher reality may be that there are genuinely incompatible dimensions to the Irish scene.

What does seem obvious enough is that any successful program would have to be characterized by its pragmatism, but true believers do not make good pragmatists. As the final year of Michael Collins's life suggests, pragmatism is too readily seen as equivalent to treachery. Such an outlook has been true of republicans and loyalists alike.

Sinn Fein's Bernadette O'Hagan at the 1996 Easter Commemoration at Holy Cross Cemetery outside of San Francisco. Photo by Douglass McFerran.

Members of the 1996 Noraid tour in Belfast. Photo by Douglass McFerran.

The Bogside, Derry, on the eve of the Apprentice Boys' march. Photo by Douglass McFerran.

The RUC station on the road to the Falls in Belfast. Photo by Douglass McFerran.

Milltown cemetery in Belfast. The tomb of a Sinn Fein worker killed by loyalists. Photo by Douglass McFerran.

At the entrance to the Bogside. A memorial to those killed on Bloody Sunday. Photo by Douglass McFerran.

Young nationalists in the Internment March coming down Falls Road. Photo by Douglass McFerran.

The City Centre in Belfast at the time of the 1996 Internment March. Photo by Douglass McFerran.

Gerry Adams, President of Sinn Fein. Photo by Adrienne McFerran.

Douglass and Adrienne McFerran with an RUC officer ordered to pose with them.

Part III

Talking with the Rebels

The "murders" were the legitimate acts of self-defence which had been forced upon the Irish people by English aggression. After two years we had begun to defend ourselves and the life of our nation. We did not initiate the war, and we did not select the battleground.
Michael Collins

7

Back to Britain

Thousands had marched in mourning all over Ireland and in the
United States, but I was the only one priviledged [sic] to stand up
for the cause ennobled by these humble men openly and defiantly
in the midst of our enemies—great as they were—with their
money, their Army, Navy, and Air Force, their lions, unicorns, and
ermine robes to hide their hangman's overalls.

Brendan Behan, *Borstal Boy*

ENGLAND AND SCOTLAND: JULY 1996

My last trip to Britain had been a very hurried one. This time, my
wife insisted, we would attempt to see more of the country. I needed
to be in Dublin at the beginning of August, but before then we would
drive through England and Scotland as proper tourists.

Shortly before we left, a TWA flight out of New York blew up over
the ocean. Immediate speculation was that terrorists had struck
again, but no group rushed forward to claim responsibility. It was
not the most auspicious beginning to our trip, especially since it was
my intention to meet with people described as terrorists in the world
press. It was marching season in Northern Ireland, and there were
anxious reports that full civil war was imminent. It was always possible, then, that my wife and I might be caught up in some new IRA
"spectacular" from the moment we entered British airspace. Even
though I thought it highly unlikely, I had completed my revisions of

the first two sections of this book just in case I was wrong and ironically met my end while researching what the IRA was all about.

The day we arrived, headlines in the London papers announced
that expert opinion was leaning to the theory that indeed a bomb
had caused the first of the two explosions that broke apart the TWA
plane. There were the usual posters in the terminal alerting patrons
to be on their guard against terrorism by promptly reporting pack-
ages left unattended. Apart from this, I found no evidence of height-
ened security. We were welcomed into the country as tourists on
holiday, and we quickly lost ourselves in the polyglot crowds throng-
ing the London streets. I tried to imagine how easily I could have
come here for some dark deed to strike at the seat of English power. I
kept coming back to the thought of Edward O'Brien getting on a
London bus with his bomb. How easy it would be for a hundred or a
thousand like him to land here just as I did, then lose themselves on
the streets until their moment came. What would make London safe
from them?

The next day I had something of an answer. According to the
Times, John Patrick Crawley, an American ex-marine who had served
in the elite Seals almost twenty years ago, had just been arrested in
London as a member of an IRA active service unit. He had moved to
the Dublin area some years before, and supposedly he now had been
planning to carry out operations ordered by the hard-liners in the
IRA's Southern Command. I found myself wondering about a number of things that I was fairly sure I would not find discussed in the
papers. Was this one of the individuals who had carried out the
Dockside bombing? Had he been identified through astute police
work? Or had he been given up by an informer? Did his arrest mean
that IRA actions in England were so compromised that I no longer
had to worry about being caught up in one of them?

One thing I did find interesting was that, unlike Eddie O'Brien,
Crawley was hardly the amateur warrior. For one thing, he was
trained to handle sophisticated explosives. If there were even a few
more like him in the half-dozen or so active service units presumed
to be operating in England, the IRA had come much closer to match-
ing the skills of the best British soldiers. Stopping its efforts would be
difficult without compromising the degree of personal freedom
taken for granted by the average Englishman, if not by the average
Irishman from the six counties. And that, of course, might well be the
point of the campaign. In the mind of the bombers, a taste of internment or personal experience of the Diplock courts would rapidly
wean someone from London or Manchester away from the idea that

the British in Northern Ireland were the honest guarantors of law and order.

There were the mandatory tourist stops. One was Blenheim Palace, home of the Churchills. Like Lord Mountbatten, Winston Churchill is a hero to the English but not to the Irish. As home secretary, he had supported the Home Rule Bill early in the century, but he failed to appreciate the danger coming from militant Unionists such as Edward Carson. In 1920, at the height of Michael Collins's war against England, when loyalist brutality against Catholics had already triggered comparisons with the pogroms of Russia, he had suggested arming the Protestants of the six counties and charging them with maintaining law and order throughout Ireland. As Jonathan Bardon tells the story, the response of one legal expert was that in Belfast "the Protestants would reduce the Catholics to a state of terror," and in Tyrone "there would be unceasing and unending civil war."

Another stop was the cathedral in Canterbury, where the Anglican archbishop had angered devout Orangemen by kneeling in prayer with Pope John Paul II on the spot where his most famous predecessor had been assassinated on the orders of Henry II. A reminder of the Tudor attitude toward anyone from the church who dared stand against a king was the plaque marking the place where a shrine to Thomas à Becket had been demolished on orders of Henry VIII.

In York at the Minster I found the rather unexpected resting place for the ashes of General Sir John Maxwell, the man who had ordered the execution of the leaders of the Easter Uprising. It was in front of a statue of the Virgin Mary, and it was the only memorial in that part of the crypt. He had died in February 1929, and his ashes were joined by those of his wife when she died some months later.

In Scotland, I made it a point to ask anyone I could about attitudes toward independence. A young store manager reminded me, as someone Irish, that we were all Celts. In ten years there would be independence, he predicted. In a past referendum, three-quarters of those voting had favored it, but Margaret Thatcher's government had ignored the results. No Tories had been elected from Scotland, he insisted.

A woman who had given us directions echoed this feeling. Her example was the fact that no one ever cheered for England in the soccer matches, no matter whom they were playing. "We're all Scottish, not English," she said. I thought of the irony that determined Ulstermen, who flew the Union Jack so proudly, insisted on a Scottish identity as though this did make them more English.

I asked a guide at Edinburgh Castle about his own feelings. "They have tried to treat us as a wee province," he said, "but it didn't work before and it won't work now." Asked about the feeling for Scots Gaelic as an expression of national identity, he responded that study of the language was just not given support by the government. He had used it with his grandmother way to the north when he was a child, but then he had almost completely forgotten it.

An even more interesting remark came from another tour guide attempting to explain the signficance of the crown jewels—the Honours. Queen Elizabeth could never wear them. "Because she is the sovereign of the United Kingdom, she is our queen, but she is not the queen of Scotland," he stated rather fiercely. I was not sure I completely saw the logic of this, but I found the suggestion that someday Scotland might again have a monarch of its own a good expression of the depth of antagonism between the Scots and their neighbors to the south.

There was no feeling that there had to be a violent resolution of differences, as there had been in Ireland, but there seemed to be a strong conviction that in time there would be a different political structure. Our innkeeper in Edinburgh, commenting on the constant rounds of marching by which Ulstermen marked English victory in their area, pointed out that no one found it important to celebrate the battle at Culloden, in which "Bonnie Prince Charlie," who might have become Charles III had he succeeded, was defeated by the English under Lord Cumberland, just as his grandfather James II had been defeated by William of Orange.

In Carlisle, just south of the border, another innkeeper remarked that people from Scotland or Ireland listed themselves as Scottish or Irish, yet visitors from different parts of England invariably said they were British rather than English. Herself a Scot, she regarded this as something quite curious, as though the English had not quite come to grips with their identity apart from being the conquerors. If she was correct, it helped explain why the English looked at separation movements in Scotland or Wales with such antagonism. Dismember "Britain" and what would they be now? It reminded me of the manner in which, during discussions of ethnic identity in my classes, it was whites who found it so difficult to accept categorization into any specific group—to be "hyphenated Americans"—while blacks and Hispanics not only accepted it for themselves but had come to regard it as a matter of pride to do so.

BELFAST AND DUBLIN: JULY 30

Returning to Ireland, I felt a certain measure of apprehension. On July 12, the anniversary of the Battle of the Boyne, Ulstermen march in celebration. This year there had been a disturbing confrontation close to the town of Portadown, not far from Belfast. After crossing a bridge over the River Bann at a place called Drumcree, marching bands and squads of well-dressed Orangemen with traditional bowler hats and sashes over their shoulders were to proceed through a Catholic area on Garvaghy Street. Historically this had been an opportunity for the marchers to taunt the Catholics with the reminder of the Protestant victory that had effectively sealed the fate of the northern counties. The Bann itself was historically the line of demarcation between Catholic and Protestant areas, with anyone west of the Bann seen in second-class status.

A year before, there had been a special effort by the RUC to redirect the march, and throughout the year there had been considerable rhetoric about "the spirit of Drumcree." Again the decision was not to allow the traditional march. I had followed the events carefully in the week before I left for London, and like anyone else with a television I could see the RUC attempting to barricade Garvaghy Road against determined Orangemen. The possibility of uncontainable violence increased when loyalist supporters poured into the area, even bringing an armored bulldozer that might plow through the defenses. In the days before the key march, in several counties there were numerous incidents in which both sides used firebombs, and near Portadown a Catholic cabdriver was found shot to death. The main highways in the Belfast area were closed, and the north seemed on the verge of a cataclysm. The RUC commander then reversed himself, and a relatively small group of marchers was allowed to proceed rather solemnly through the area.

Three weeks later I expected something close to martial law. Instead I found life going on as normal, with the police and military virtually invisible in cities and towns that not long before had seen so much violence. I was beginning to wonder whether the media had exaggerated the precariousness of the situation.

At the airport in Belfast we rented a car and drove down to Dublin. Near the border, in south Armagh, I finally did see a squad of troopers marching along the highway, well spread out to limit casualties in case of an ambush. It was in an area where the Tricolor was openly on display, various signs indicated the RUC was unwelcome, and a list of local men held as prisoners of war was painted on a wall. I was not sure just what statement the patrol was supposed to be making, although the men themselves might definitely prefer being out in the open to the alternative of being penned in the military barracks.

There were several military checkpoints at which it was posted that no photography was allowed, but we were simply waved through until we entered the Republic.

At our hotel in Dublin I talked with the young woman at the desk. Tourism from the north had completely stopped, she told us. For herself she found all the protests on both sides rather stupid, but her boyfriend held very different views and had a strong admiration for Gerry Adams.

The newspapers were reporting that the oldest man in England had just died. His particular claim to fame was that as a Welsh fusilier he had assisted in one of the arrests of Eamon de Valera and spent an entire night in conversation with him.

COUNTY WEXFORD: JULY 31

I found myself attempting to understand what had motivated young Eddie O'Brien from Gorey in County Wexford. In the city of Wexford there was a memorial to the pikemen of 1798, but otherwise, as in Dublin, most of the landmarks—the public buildings and the larger mansions—were evidence of the Protestant Ascendancy. As in Hawaii, it seemed the local economy was sustained by tourism. Unemployment, I knew, was still very high, and surprisingly few teenagers actually got their "leaving certificates"—what we would think of as high school diplomas. Drugs and the criminal groups connected with their import and distribution were supposedly a major problem in Dublin, and I wondered just how different things were in the more rural areas.

I tried to imagine Eddie O'Brien as a youngster with little chance of moving ahead in life. He had told his family that he was a laborer in Glasgow when actually he was hiding out in London, another young Irishman not known to the authorities as having any link with the IRA. Rightly or not, he might blame his own limited opportunities on British oppression, and so find himself identifying with the rebels of two centuries before. He had been given a chance to be a modern-day pikeman, and he took it.

At his funeral all the paraphernalia of republicanism had been banned, but I wondered how many youngsters in the area were ready to take his place now that he had received his apotheosis as one more in the line of IRA men killed on active service. How many of them might even now be reading Brendan Behan's autobiographical *Borstal Boy*, an account of his time in custody after being arrested as a sixteen-year-old IRA bomber in Liverpool following the deadly explosion at Coventry in 1939, and imagining themselves continuing the war?

CORK: AUGUST 1

Before leaving Los Angeles, I had been given the name of a man whom I would later hear described as possibly one of the most important figures in the unwritten history of the Irish struggle. I'll call him Francis. I did not have a number for him, but I did have the name of an organization he had begun in order to facilitate contacts between Protestant and Catholic young people. The name of the group was in the Cork phone book, and around nine in the morning I set out to find the address. If he was not there, I might at least have a chance to talk with people who worked with him.

At the door of one of the blocks of flats converted to commercial use, I rang the intercom and mentioned my contact in California. After the buzzer rang, I pushed open the door and made my way up several flights of stairs to a set of rooms converted to offices and overflowing with cartons of books and papers. Francis proved to be about my age, a robust Irishman who greeted me warmly and sent an assistant to fetch us coffee and scones. For the next two hours we talked about a range of subjects, with Francis repeatedly apologizing that he was not letting me do a proper interview because he was telling so many stories. For my part, I kept trying to reassure him that this was far better than any structured interview. He was giving me an insider's picture of current republicanism that was just what I needed.

As it turned out, Francis had come under fire from the expatriate Irish in San Francisco because of his current work with the Protestants from Northern Ireland. He had been visiting California and was giving a talk about his work to one of the activist groups. A couple of men came in twenty minutes late. They had been drinking, and they were feeling particularly belligerent. First off, Francis refused to repeat what he had said so far, and this incited them to challenge his credentials as someone representing the republican cause.

"Wolfe Tone died two hundred years ago," one of them said, as though the age in which those loyal to the ideal of an independent Ireland could associate with Protestants had died at the same time.

Francis cited the support for his work that he had from Gerry Adams. "Well, Adams isn't here to explain himself," was the reply.

Francis shook his head. "So I told them that if Wolfe Tone and Gerry Adams were not good enough republicans for them, I had nothing else to say." He went on to explain that he had given up drinking many years before, and he saw the intransigence of these two men to be as much a product of the bottle as of any misguided loyalty. It was difficult to say which bothered him more, the challenge he had been given or the fact that those challenging him were playing right to a familiar stereotype.

"That's the image people have of the Irish, you know. We're all drunks, so of course we do not have to be taken seriously. The British had to rule us for our own good. Did you ever see the way we were depicted in the British magazines from the last century on—simian features and carrying a jug?"

I was quite familiar with the often savage political cartoons appearing in magazines such as *Punch* and given insightful analysis in R. F. Foster's essay "Paddy and Mr. Punch." This was the image that still survived in the typical rendition of the leprechaun as a rotund figure in a tight jacket and britches. On the stage in England and America, a familiar source of humor was the stock Irishman with his pipe and his jug of poteen, his fractured English and his peculiar conceptions of history and geography. In vaudeville, just like the watermelon-eating black boy who would do a fast shuffle to delight the white folks, the well-lubricated Irishman was brought on to tell a tall story or do a jig.

"There was a store here that was selling souvenirs for the tourists. They included towels with the cartoons of drunken Irishmen and those phrases that are supposed to be cute. I went to the clerk and asked him if he thought that was what we all were—stupid and drunk. He said no, so I asked him if he thought the cartoon was about him or about me or about anyone else he knew. Again he said no. So I told him I wanted those souvenirs removed from display because they were insulting. He said he was only the clerk. All right, he could meet with the owner, but I would be back the next day, and if the towels were still there, I would have a picket line set up outside the shop. It made as much sense for an Irishman to display that type of thing as for a Jewish shopkeeper to sell souvenirs with cartoons about people with big noses who were tight with their money.

"The next day the stuff was gone. Now the clerk had said we should have a sense of humor and be able to laugh at ourselves, but I don't agree. This isn't what we are, but it's the way people who have it

in for us would like us to be seen. Making someone appear ridicu-
lous is part of the process of dehumanization."

Francis was a man who laughed easily, and he certainly did not
come off as a rigid apostle of what has come to be called political
correctness. His emphasis was on dignity, the sense of personal
worth that any stereotype assaults. The world of those in power had
a reason to encourage its members to think of the powerless in terms
of drunken Irishmen, stingy Jews, stupid blacks, greedy Arabs, lazy
Mexicans, whooping Indians, and so on. Subjugated peoples were
seen as buffoons, so part of the process of escaping subjugation had
to be a clear rejection of all such buffoonery.

I asked how the IRA saw drinking and drug use. In England I had
heard repeatedly that the IRA was all about drugs and guns and money,
as though Belfast and Derry were like the Chicago of Al Capone. Francis
explained that partying was not allowed the individual in an active
service unit—the volunteer in the strict sense. A man could either drink
or be on active duty, but not both. Saying that the IRA dealt in drugs was
a convenient media account, a way of explaining away the actual
support the IRA had in the Catholic community. The truth of the matter
was that the IRA was deeply concerned with keeping the drug dealer
out, not to take his place but to protect the community from problems
even worse than alcoholism.

We spent quite a bit of time discussing the media. I was already
coming to understand that the men and women involved with the
IRA were not at all what I would have expected after seeing Jeff
Bridges and Tommy Lee Jones in *Blown Away* or Harrison Ford's adversaries in *Patriot Games* or Miranda Richardson in *The Crying
Game*—and I could only guess what Brad Pitt would be like in a
movie, still to be released, about a volunteer on the run. Ireland did
not yet have its Coppola or Scorsese to portray the sheer ordinari-
ness of the individuals caught up in a continuing state of rebellion—
the so-called Long War that had already lasted a quarter-century and
that might last a quarter-century more.

Hollywood exaggerated the volunteer in the same way it had exaggerated the gunslinger in its Westerns, only there was a political subtext here that was not present in all the oaters about Wyatt Earp or
Billy the Kid. For the media there had to be something pathological
about the Irish gunman or bomber, something that could account
for the Troubles without suggesting that America's great ally might be
to blame and that the United States itself was cooperating by not
censuring Britain's systematic human rights violations in the north.

Again Francis had a story. There was a young woman who had been sentenced to prison in the Republic for her involvement with an IRA unit. She was sent across the country to the Cork area, where she did not have any family or friends. Francis was asked to look after her, visiting her in prison and seeing that she had whatever would be allowed. On the day of her release he brought a camera and insisted on having her pose by the gates.

"She was a beautiful redhead, a girl that could be a model. This wasn't some street tough, but that would be how the media would like to have you think of the women from the IRA."

I told Francis about the girl I have named Jennifer Pearse, the young electronics engineer who had served time for allegedly conspiring to develop high-tech weapons to bring down British helicopters. I had been struck by the fact that Jennifer was not the hard-edged woman I might have imagined. At the commemoration I had attended the past Easter, Bernadette O'Hagan, herself a former inmate at a women's prison in Armagh and the wife and mother of volunteers, was a sweet little lady who could have been serving tea and cakes at a church social. Neither Jennifer nor Mrs. O'Hagan fit the Hollywood image of the dedicated, semicrazed "terrorist." The problem was that it was more convenient to accept the Hollywood image, in that it absolved Americans of complicity in the Troubles.

During our conversation Francis had a number of phone calls. Shortly before I had to leave, a call came in about setting up lodging for a man from Belfast. Francis explained that the guest was a rather well-known Protestant paramilitary, one of the fighters in the Ulster Volunteer Force. The man was extremely apprehensive about coming to the Cork area, where the IRA, even though outlawed, is still strong.

"I'm trying to reassure him. Of course there are some men here who want to meet with him, but they're being friendly."

I tried to picture the situation. In March, Father Timoney in Belfast told me about meetings arranged at Clonard Monastery, on the border between Catholic and Protestant areas in West Belfast. They had been tense at the beginning, but over a period of time, veterans of the conflict between the IRA and INLA and a number of Protestant paramilitary groups had been able to establish a measure of communication that in part explained the relative quiet in the north even after the IRA declared an end to its cease-fire. Later I would hear that there were still ongoing exchanges with loyalists staying over in a Catholic area and republicans visiting Protestant strongholds.

What Francis was doing, I realized, reached far beyond bringing Protestant and Catholic youngsters together. He was also reaching out to their parents in an enterprise that might best be compared with having diehard KKK men share a barbecue with folks from the NAACP. I also understood how he had managed to antagonize some of the people in America who, far from the scene in which loyalists and republicans are finding common ground, took offense at this ecumenical approach.

DUBLIN: AUGUST 2

Driving in England had allowed me to get used to driving on the left, but in Ireland I found that the greatest source of frustration was that manner in which a regular highway (a dual-lane carriageway) turned into a series of turns on narrow streets in the towns through which we passed. The Irish government had managed, according to a news article I read, to bring forty-two percent of its roads up to international standards. I was quickly discovering what it was like to be on the remaining fifty-eight percent, especially in the more scenic areas that my wife demanded we visit as compensation for the time I would be involved in my interviews.

One thing I soon realized was that the quaint Ireland of nine-teenth-century ways had already disappeared. Adequate paved roads linked even the smallest of villages, and there was a disconcerting similarity among them. B&Bs were everywhere, the news agents had papers from all over Ireland and England, there were video stores and pizza parlors, and the Guinness people had managed to franchise their pubs everywhere. One of the most familiar signs was the warning that a creamery exit was ahead, and I learned to watch for the trucks carrying rich dairy products. And everywhere there were sheep, raised not so much for their meat as for their wool.

One statistic that is still amazing is that Ireland holds fewer people today than it did a century and a half ago. Certainly there is no longer the horrifying poverty and degradation that accompanied overcrowding, and at present Ireland has the fastest-growing economy in Europe. What I did not see, however, was the evidence of industrialization so apparent elsewhere. This was still an essentially rural country that concentrated a third of its population in the city of Dublin, and even there it was hard to see how the money came in apart from tourism and the Guinness and the wool sweaters.

The Irish papers have reason to express concern for the future, in that fewer young people are going on for higher education, and

drugs and organized crime are becoming epidemic. Even though
out-migration is now being balanced by individuals returning to Ireland, especially to live out their retirement years, the stasis in population is not something that bodes well for competition in a
high-tech era, since it is the most talented who are leaving for greater
opportunities in England or Europe or the United States. People survive because there is a generous welfare program, but there is also an
increasing strain on the economy as the average age of Irish citizens
increases.

At the same time American business analysts have predicted that
Ireland in another decade will be the Singapore of Europe, with
cheap land and labor, a well-educated workforce, and a government
that is encouraging new investments. Perhaps they are right, but I
had not seen the level of prosperity that is being cited. Possibly it is
just that I have no basis for comparison, since I was not in Ireland
ten or twenty years ago.

One of the most striking things was the music I heard in the various shops and pubs. In Kinsale, while nursing a pint of Guinness, I
nearly burst out laughing when I heard Jimmy Durante singing that a
kiss is just a kiss. True, it was a song featured in the film *Sleepless in
Seattle*, but it seemed so out of place in this scenic harbor village.
The more I listened, though, the more I realized I was in a time warp
of sorts. Everywhere I was hearing the standards of twenty to fifty
years ago, newly discovered and played incessantly. This was not altogether unpleasant. There was certainly none of the rap that assaulted the ears in trendy American stores, and somehow it did seem
fitting to hear Patsy Cline and Roy Orbison in this land of cows and sheep.

In Dublin there were two stories in that day's newspapers that
were particularly interesting. A few weeks earlier a bomb had gone
off at a Protestant-owned hotel in Enniskillen in County Fermanaugh, but now the place was being reopened. To that point no
group had taken credit for the bombing, and the lingering suspicion
among some republicans was that the bombing was actually set up
by the British to justify Protestant retaliation against the IRA.

The other article was about the man who had written the best-
selling *The Nemesis File* under the name of Paul Bruce. "Bruce" had
claimed to be a British soldier recruited for undercover work with the
Special Air Services in the north, and he had provided a harrowing
tale of a death squad that finally was ordered to kill randomly on the
streets of West Belfast, in order to provoke a confrontation between
Catholics and Protestants that would justify stronger British intervention. He had been taken into custody by the RUC just the day

before, but now he was released and the official story was that his book was a hoax. Republicans again were skeptical.

A small bit of knowledge came my way very unexpectedly in a shop specializing in old books. A title caught my eye: *The Green Book*. It was a volume published in 1862, and the subtitle was *Reading Made Easy of the Irish Statutes*. Later I asked someone connected with the IRA whether this was the basis for the title of the volume put out for volunteers, and I was told that indeed it was. After all, the IRA did consider itself the only legitimate government of Ireland, and apparently someone familiar with the old text that included all the laws set out by the British government found its title appropriate for what in effect were statutes set out by the Army Council.

8

The Marching Season

These are not easy times for Unionism or for loyalism, assailed on every side by enemies within and without. Not since the stirring days of the Home Rule crisis of 1912–14 has there been such a sustained and unrelenting campaign to detach Ulster from the United Kingdom and incorporate it into an all-Ireland scenario.

Orangemen and Orangewomen are, as always, in the vanguard of resistance to any weakening of the position of loyal Ulster and they will be parading their loyalties and principles on the greatest day in the loyalist calendar.

Orange Standard, July 1996

DUBLIN: AUGUST 3

Summer is marching season in the north of Ireland. From June through August, Protestant groups ritually acknowledge a number of anniversaries, the most important of which is the twelfth of July, marking the defeat of James II by the Protestant William III of Orange ("King Billy") in the Battle of the Boyne. Elaborate processions make their way through city streets, and bands from all over the Protestant areas of the north converge for special remembrances. They are loud and colorful and a source of pride for Ulstermen, like an American Fourth of July parade magnified and repeated.

According to a 1996 study prepared for the University of Ulster's Centre for the Study of Conflict (*Parade and Protest: A Discussion of*

Parading Disputes in Northern Ireland), there are now, on average, twenty-five hundred parades a year by loyalists. Republicans also march, but at only about a tenth the rate. The total number of marches has increased over the last decade, and for participants— loyalist or republican—they are an expression of national identity, while for those on the opposing side they are offensive displays calculated to demean those who hold a contrary position. Almost predictably they hold the potential for violence, particularly when loyalists demand a supposedly historic right to march in what has now become a Catholic neighborhood.

I had come to Ireland at this time to take part in one march in Belfast that marked the anniversary of the widespread internment by which British authorities had hoped to break the IRA in the early 1970s. For a number of years this had been an opportunity for Noraid, the American-based group raising funds for the families of those interned, to sponsor what was billed as a fact-finding tour through the north. The group would convene in Dublin, then be bused through the northern counties and end up in Belfast on August 12 to take part in the march. As part of my research I had decided to meet up with the group at the beginning and the end of their trip. In the meantime I would continue driving through other parts of the island.

At midmorning I exited the DART train that had taken me from our hotel in Dun Laoghaire (pronounced *dun lary*) just south of the city, to the Pearse Street station. A few blocks walk along Pearse Street away from the city center, I came to the pub known as Widow Scallan's, allowed to open early because of its proximity to a train station. I had come here the night before to have a pint of Guinness with my wife, but then the crowd had seemed a fairly rough group of young workingmen; now there were mostly senior citizens—old-age pensioners—having an early drink and looking all the worse for it.

Gradually the leaders of our small group appeared. Bill Quinn from Kansas City was one of the dedicated Noraid leaders, and we talked about mutual acquaintances from the San Francisco area. My surname was already familiar from Internet postings about the July 20 demonstration held in various cities against British authorities, who appeared to have capitulated to the loyalist threat of violence in Portadown and then turned around and attacked nationalist protesters in a number of cities. My son had led the demonstration in Los Angeles, even getting a few minutes of television coverage, and I justified my presence here as his representative for the march coming up in Belfast.

There were close to three dozen Americans who had flown over. For about four hundred dollars they would share a bus for ten days and spend their nights as guests of various nationalist families. The number had held steady over recent years, although when the tour had first started a dozen years earlier, there had been five times as many participants. Several were like Bill in making this an annual event, but most were individuals who had only recently become involved in Irish activism.

A portly older man appeared and was seated as a special guest of honor. His name, I heard, was Joe Cahill. Later I read more about him, and what I learned was that he was one of the so-called Forties men, veterans of an older IRA come back to work with the Provos in Belfast as the Troubles got under way. Joe had been imprisoned several times, had come close to being hanged in 1943 for the murder of a police officer, and had survived to become a member of the Army Council and one of the founders of Noraid. At the time of the cease-fire in 1994, according to Tim Pat Coogan, he had been selected to come to the United States to bring hard-line Irish-Americans in Noraid over to Gerry Adams's point of view but had been denied a visa. An American present that morning jokingly referred to him as an IRA "godfather," perhaps as much to note how his girth resembled Marlon Brando's as to comment on his biography.

Joe welcomed us briefly, as did a Sinn Fein councillor from Belfast whom I'll call Sean Reilly. As the group left to prepare for a tour of the city, I had a chance to talk more with Sean, explaining, as I did, how I was building a book out of conversations such as this. I also explained how I usually preferred pseudonyms and might well condense several figures into one for the purpose of my narrative. He agreed to chat, and I tried to probe more deeply than I had yet done into the thinking of individuals who, if not themselves IRA men, remained always quite close to those who were.

The inevitable question was whether there was a split within the IRA. Certainly the press had speculated about this, and the timing of the end of the cease-fire and the Canary Wharf bombing had added to the impression that Gerry Adams and Sinn Fein had been found wanting by hard-liners on the Army Council. Sean insisted vehemently that there was no split and certainly no intentional effort to embarrass Adams. Sinn Fein, he insisted, worked for a strictly political solution while the IRA worked for both a political and a military solution. The goals of the two groups were not at all incompatible.

This was the official line I had heard a number of times already. The media in particular had made much of the fact that Adams would not condemn the IRA bombings in England, and official statements from the IRA's Army Council, such as the Easter message I heard delivered at the commemoration in San Francisco, seemed to go out of their way to insist in return that resumption of military action was not a condemnation of Adams. Both groups repeated the idea of their respective autonomy, despite the fact that Sinn Fein is almost invariably presented as the IRA's political wing. If I were to accept this, it is as though there are two roads up the mountain, with some preferring one for themselves but wishing the best to climbers not on the same path. At best it seemed naive. At worst it was a desperate effort to paper over the differences between well-known figures such as Adams and McGuinness and the otherwise invisible men who comprised a majority on the Army Council.

Sean was an interesting man quite apart from his role as one of those elected to city government from Sinn Fein. He had lost both his brother and his son to sectarian violence, and for that reason I might have expected someone consumed with a passion for revenge. Instead I found an oddly gentle man to whom it was entirely natural to recite a poem of his own in answer to a question.

One of my questions was deeply personal. Young people like my son and his friend Kevin Doherty expressed a strong commitment to the Irish cause that included an acceptance of the bombing campaign. That worried me, in that I feared the tendency to romanticize rebellion and a corresponding impatience with the often torturous paths of strictly political activity. "There is nothing romantic about a revolution," Sean said, going on to lines he had written about death in the streets. It even bothered him, he said, when would-be patriots started in with all the old IRA songs about the glory of dying for Ireland.

What of the future? Would the prospect of a Labour victory in the next election suggest a change in British policy?

"Tory Major or Tory Blair, there will not be a difference. I wish we had Margaret Thatcher back, since at least she would have stood up to the opposition in Portadown. Major simply capitulated."

After our conversation I walked back through Dublin's center. I had some time before I was to meet up with my wife, so I took the opportunity to tour the inside of the government offices just down from the National Gallery. In the room where the Irish Council met, a guard appointed to see to our tour group waited patiently while I wrote down the names of the individuals in the portraits hung on the walls. The group began with Patrick Sarsfield, the Jacobite commander who had held out against William of Orange in Limerick until forced to surrender and sign the Treaty of Limerick, and ended with the formidable Countess Constance Markievicz, who might be thought of as the Irish Betsy Ross in that she had fashioned the original flag of the republic proclaimed during the Easter Rebellion. The revolutionaries Wolfe Tone and Padraic Pearse shared walls with the politicians Daniel O'Connell and Charles Parnell, and I had to wonder how the men and women who sit in this chamber really feel about these now legendary figures. How much do they identify with the message implicit in the magnificent stained glass window at the head of the main landing that depicts the four ancient kingdoms—the "four fields" of rebel Irish songs? How committed are they to the articles in the Irish constitution that call for a unified country?

An obvious problem is that for three-quarters of a century the government of Eire—what was once the Free State and then the Republic of Ireland—has had to deal with the consequences of Michael Collins's concessions ending the Anglo-Irish War. Collins himself died by an IRA man's bullet in 1922, and two years later open hostilities ended with the regular Irish army brought under the clear control of the existing government. From then on, what was called the Irish Republican Army was an outlaw group—modern versions of the "Wild Geese," the Jacobite soldiers who had fought against William of Orange and then continued a life of banditry after their defeat—not just in the British-occupied counties of the north but in the rest of the island as well. But for the IRA, with its Army Council elected not by the people of Ireland but by another group of senior republicans, the story was that the elected officials meeting in Dublin had no more authority in Ireland than the elected officials meeting in London.

When I had first begun meeting with republicans in San Francisco, I had to ask myself whether these men and women, who seemed to identify so strongly with the events of 1916, were that much different from the Russian émigrés who used to gather in various cities and plot the overthrow of the Communist regime that took power in 1917. Now that I was meeting with republicans in Ireland itself, I was coming to appreciate that the situation was a far more complex one than I had originally thought. The principal reason was that the situation in the north continued a history of anti-Catholic bigotry that had nearly precipitated civil war during the discussion of home rule in the period between 1912 and 1914 (the "stirring days" of present-day Orangeman editorializing). The Irish Republic could establish a situation of normalcy in which sectarian differences were irrelevant, but this has so far evaded the powers-that-be in the northern counties. To say that the IRA created the problems of the north is quite simply to ignore the actual history of the area, but given these problems, the IRA, or at least its surrogates in Sinn Fein, must be recognized as a necessary party in any discussion of their resolution.

What the marching season was bringing out yet again was that the old motto of "no surrender" dating from the resistance of Derry besieged by James II still dominates the thinking of many of those who represent the wealth and power of modern-day Ulster. Much of it reflects a fear of a supposedly theocratic Irish Republic that would suppress Protestants in the same way Protestants have suppressed Catholics. It is an image of the Catholic Church that is almost ludicrous to today's rebellious Catholics, but it is consistently reinforced in the preaching of Ian Paisley and others who share his view. The closest parallel I can find is in the vision of Catholics running the government held by some extremist groups in the United States, as in the flyers I have seen in Los Angeles that purport to explain the linkage between the Vatican, Moscow, and Jewish bankers. (My opinion, of course, can be readily discounted in that, as an ex-Jesuit, I am really part of the conspiracy!)

Given this hard-line Protestant view, someone like Gerry Adams does not stand much chance of being heard fairly. The failure to recognize any distinction between Sinn Fein and the IRA itself only complicates the picture. For the dedicated Orangeman, Adams has to be a bald-faced liar when he talks about peace and the IRA continues to set off its bombs. A poll sponsored by the *Irish Times* and taken not long after I was in Ireland indicated that Adams was seen negatively by three-quarters of Protestant respondents and by a quarter of Catholic respondents. In a cross-community scoring he fell way behind Ian Paisley and David Trimble in terms of approval of his leadership. It was not a statistic that Adams could have been pleased with, but what is worse is that it seemingly justified his continued exclusion from the peace talks that he had helped to bring about.

DERRY AND OMAGH: AUGUST 7

We spent several more days as tourists in the west of Ireland, finally arriving at the rustic town of Buncrana in County Donegal, not far from the border. The London papers, which were like the Irish papers in their effort to avoid libel suits by using colorful pseudonyms for individuals who might be involved in criminal activity but had not yet been brought to justice, were discussing the fact that someone referred to as "King Rat" in Portadown was at odds with the leadership of the Protestant paramilitaries because of his alleged participation in a sectarian killing. There was also discussion of a new book created from the diaries of Superintendent Ian Phoenix of MI5, one of the men involved in covert operations in Northern Ireland.

I had called the Sinn Fein councillor I'll refer to as Rory McBride in County Tyrone. Rory was Thomas's longtime friend and my chief contact in the north, and again I needed to set up an interview. Thomas himself was visiting his family in County Fermanaugh, and I called him as well. Both men said the situation was quiet for the present, but there was still the concern that everything might explode as the marching season proceeded to its climax in Derry in another few days. A key issue there had been the unwillingness of representatives from the Catholics in the Bogside community just to the west of the city center to allow an Orange march along the city walls overlooking the Bogside. So far negotiations seemed stalemated, and after the near violence at Portadown there was justifiable concern that this would be the occasion for uncontrolled violence as incoming thousands of Orangemen confronted the citizens of what now had become a predominantly Catholic city.

We spent the early part of the morning at the Grianan of Aileach, where supposedly St. Patrick had baptized the first O'Neill king to convert to Christianity. This was an enclosed area with ramparted walls that commanded a magnificent view of the Inishowen peninsula jutting out between Lough Swilly and Lough Foyle. Then we drove the short distance to County Derry and the area of Ireland still a part of the United Kingdom.

After our trip through Armagh to Dublin, I had been expecting a strong military presence, and I had my passport ready along with my cover story that I was an innocent American tourist exploring his ancestral roots in the north. With all the discussion about the potential violence in Derry with the traditional Apprentice Boys' march at the weekend, I was ready for intensive interrogation with every piece of luggage checked for weapons or explosives. As it happened, there was a solitary Irish policeman at the Donegal side of the border; he waved everyone through in both directions with no particular concern. There was absolutely no sign of a military buildup all the way into the city, where we parked in a multistory structure identical to what I was used to in Southern California. We exited into a thoroughly modern shopping mall and then what is known as the Diamond, the heart of the old walled city.

My wife happily went shopping, and I took the opportunity to walk the walls surrounding the old area. I did chat with a member of the RUC, who said it was not advisable to be here on Friday evening but that, yes, everything was now quite normal. At the lovely little St. Augustine's Church, which is accessible from that part of the wall overlooking the Bogside, I met with a charming gentleman whom I took to be part of the team managing this Church of Ireland chapel. He pointed out over the Catholic area of the Bogside and the Creggan, with their famous republican murals and the Tricolor much in evidence, and commented that the people there would not really favor reunification. The benefits, such as the unemployment funds, they received from the British government were far superior to those they would get in the Republic, and they knew this.

Meeting up with my wife, I took her back to the steps leading up to the view of the Bogside. As we got there, we were met by an armored Rover and a group of well-armed RUC that had just pulled up. Trusting my luck, I got my camera ready and asked the officer in command, the only one not in a flak jacket and carrying a weapon, whether it would be all right to take a picture. Smiling, he took my camera and ordered a young woman with her rifle to stand alongside us in front of the Rover while he himself took the picture.

Afterward we talked, and I was asked whether I was a drinking man. Assuring him that I had been known to bend the elbow, he recommended a trip to the Bushmill's distillery in County Antrim. Definitely we had to see the Giant's Causeway, one of the great natural wonders of the world, and the distillery was just down the road. When I asked about the potential for violence at the weekend, he said with a fair amount of passion that everything would be all right if people would just obey the law. It was a friendly conversation, chilled only when I pointed out that my surname was not Scottish, as he had imagined, but Irish—from Antrim itself—and I was Catholic. Or maybe I just imagined the chill when he glanced at his watch and said he had to get about his duties.

We again walked on the wall, and my wife took more pictures of the Bogside. Then we walked through the gate down into the Catholic area. I took a photo at the memorial for those killed on Bloody Sunday in 1972 and spoke a bit with a couple who had lived in the same apartment right at the gate throughout the period of the Troubles. Once again I was impressed with how easily people seem to have accommodated to the episodic violence that created the impression outside of Ireland that this was a war zone with a constantly terrified citizenry.

We drove on to Omagh in County Tyrone. I called Rory, and we set up a dinner date for that evening. As it happened, Thomas was also in town, and I was delighted at the prospect of seeing him again in his own country.

A few hours later Rory picked us up and drove over to a restaurant that Thomas said he had heard about. Over Rory's mixed grill and my whitefish we talked more about the realities of Catholic life in an area that was so mixed and where Protestant paramilitaries were quite active. Rory, whom I had earlier read about as an activist opposing the development of a uranium mining operation in the region, began talking about the circumstances that many years before had led to his time in a British jail as a remand prisoner.

It began, he said, with a request from the RUC. Word was out that one of the loyalist paramilitaries in the area had been marked for death by the IRA for some particular transgression. The intended target claimed he had not done what he was accused of. As a Sinn Fein politician, perhaps Rory would be able to contact the IRA on the man's behalf.

"So I met with the man himself to get his side of the story, and I believed him. Then I got hold of the local leaders of the IRA and they agreed to set up a meeting. I took the fellow to a room where he could tell the IRA what he had told me, and they believed him. That was supposed to be the end of it, but the next day the RUC comes to arrest me. The charge was kidnapping and false imprisonment, since I had brought the poor fellow to a place to meet with people he would not freely have met on his own, which is true in a way. It was all a setup, you see.

"At the trial, though, things did not go the way the Brits intended. They bring in the man and the judge asks if he knows me. 'Know him?' he says. 'He's the one who saved my life.' And he goes on how he would have been killed if I had not asked him to meet with the IRA to explain things. And they had to let me go, since their key witness would not tell them how I had forced him to go anywhere."

I had certainly read about savage reprisals, most notably the killing of a number of Protestant workingmen whose bus was stopped by the IRA after loyalist death squads had terrorized Catholic neighborhoods. It was a brutal act, but one of those involved is quoted as saying that it accomplished its purpose: there was a stop to the random sectarian killings by loyalists. And perhaps it was to forestall such reprisals that the sadistic leader of a loyalist group known as the Shankill Butchers was gunned down in a Protestant neighborhood, supposedly by IRA men allowed a safe passage by local paramilitaries to eliminate one of their own who had become too hot to handle.

That is not to say that killing is not part of the way of life on both sides. Certainly no one would be foolish enough not to take a death threat very seriously. Rory certainly had been threatened, and this fact made our after-dinner tour of the back roads of County Tyrone a bit more of an adventure. I had no idea of where we were going when finally he pulled into the driveway of a small house on one of the country roads. Several young boys were playing outside, and Rory asked if their father was home yet. Then he explained. The UVF had come for the man when he had not been home, and they had gunned down his wife instead. Her name was Kathleen O'Hagan, and she was pregnant with their sixth child. Rory had quickly heard of the killing and come over, only to find the area sealed off by the RUC.

Not surprisingly, the killers were never found, but what might have been a crucial piece of evidence was also missing. There were indications that the RUC had been keeping the house under camera surveillance because of the owner's suspected links to the IRA, but the camera was now gone. Rory obviously felt that the police and the gunmen had acted in collusion, either in the killing itself or in a cover-up afterward.

My wife and I saw five motherless boys awaiting the return of their dad and began to understand a bit more the harsh reality of what the middle part of the north was like. "We're west of the Bann," Rory explained, citing the river that marks the traditional boundary between areas where there is a Catholic majority and those mostly controlled by Protestants. "The money stays in the east, because that's where the power is. We don't get the same attention, whether it's in development or education or anything else. And the Protestants who are here are afraid of losing what they still have as the Catholics grow in numbers. So they try to keep us in line."

Omagh had struck me as clearly less prosperous, and I had already read about it as one of the real trouble spots. It reminded me in ways of a rural town in the southern United States at the height of the violence connected with the civil rights struggles of a generation back. Whites now outnumbered by blacks had increased the level of intimidation, not hesitating to invade a home on a back road and lynch or shoot someone they thought a troublemaker. The loyalists and the Klan did have a lot in common, not least the claim to be acting on the authority of the Bible to protect their threatened race.

We went on to another place where the mood was very different, peaceful rather than menacing. Creggan was a rustic area where the inhabitants had tried to take control of their own destiny more effectively by building a lovely retreat where rock cottages were now rented out to vacationing families. All the work had been by local men and women, using the stone and timber of the region in a marvelous instance of bootstrap economics. The Noraid tour that I had met with in Dublin had stopped off here just the day before, and I was wondering whether they were also going to Derry as the tension built in the north.

Driving back, we passed the barracks where British troops had to pass their time in what might have seemed like a state of siege. Like the RUC buildings, they were heavily secured against attack with thick concrete walls and razor-sharp barbed wire. For both the army and the police, the IRA had clearly managed to make it appear that it held the upper hand in being able to move freely through the countryside. I could not help but think of Vietnam at the height of American involvement. Even though this was part of the United Kingdom, the British citizens assigned a security role did not find it safe to be on the streets with other British citizens except in convoys. Those who had wives could not let them go shopping, and those who had children could not let them attend school off the base. It was easy enough to understand that, unable to associate freely with the Irish, they were only reinforced in a perception that these others, technically also British citizens, lacked the rights any Englishman might take for granted in his own land. It was also easy enough to understand how the Irish might agree.

Rory talked about his own time in a British jail. He had never been physically mistreated, he said, but there was every effort to break him psychologically. His own response, inculcated in every volunteer as well as in all those who might find themselves in the same position, was to avoid cooperating with his captors. There was no point interrogating him because he would not respond. There was no point demanding that he assist in his own confinement, even by sanitizing the cell when the lack of adequate facilities led to urine and feces on the floor.

"There was a time we had this screw who was all spit and polish that brought in an empty pail for our urine and another full one with water and ammonia to wash things down. He said he wanted this cell done right or we'd be sorry. One of the lads asked me what we were supposed to do. So I showed him that we pissed in the one bucket and then dumped it in the other. The screw never bothered with us again."

Rory, like so many other former prisoners, could look back almost fondly on his months of incarceration. He laughed about the time they had held a brief hunger strike. Word to call it off had finally come down, and men shouted something in Irish down the cell block. "There was one fellow there who was in solitary, and he was determined not to give in. So he gets back with us a day later and asks what it was that he heard being shouted. We told him it was the word that it was okay to eat. Well, he didn't know Irish, so he had gone on fasting. Next time I announced we were having lessons in Irish, he was the first in line."

My friend was not a big man, but his indomitable will was more than a match for the roughest types that the Brits could send against him. He had a family, but they knew as well as he did not to show fear. For Rory it was still 1916, and he continued to live in an occupied country.

I was curious about whether Sinn Fein and the IRA in the north still held as religiously to the idea that the Irish government below the border—the government that resulted from the hated treaty that had divided the island in 1921—lacked legitimacy. Rory, who admitted that he felt no special pressure to stick to a party line with me, pointed out that Gerry Adams had now started speaking of the Irish government and not just the Dublin government. To an outsider it might seem almost trivial, yet it did indicate still another pragmatic concession, and to that extent it gave some reason to believe that a peaceful resolution was still possible.

LURGAN: AUGUST 8

Rory had suggested several individuals I might want to meet in Armagh. One was an attorney named Rosemary Nelson. As it happened, her office was almost across the street from our hotel, and I was lucky enough to catch her in the late morning, probably making her go without lunch.

Rosemary was one of those people I find difficult to forget. She was a woman completely committed to representing those who were victims of British rule. Her most important case was the representation of a man named Colin Duffy, sentenced to life for his supposed involvement in the killing three years before of a British security officer, a member of the Ulster Defense Regiment named John Lynney. His appeal was coming up in September, and crucial to his case was the identity of one of those who was supposedly an eyewitness to the shooting.

Rosemary explained the proceedings of the tribunals known as Diplock courts. Whatever Americans or even people in England might think of as elementary principles of a fair trial did not hold. Witnesses were able to appear anonymously, and members of the military did not have to undergo any kind of serious cross-examination. There was no jury, since a key notion was that in Ireland an accused terrorist's peers would be unlikely to bring in a verdict of guilty. Rosemary, who appeared totally convinced of Duffy's innocence, pointed out that two of the three witnesses had been at too great a distance to identify the gunman with the accuracy that these did. The third, who was represented as a solid citizen of the area with no links to any of the paramilitaries, offered the really damning testimony that sealed Duffy's fate. It did not matter that finally the attorneys had been able to find out enough about this witness, a man named Lindsay Robb, to establish that not that long back he had given a fiery unionist speech and so might be thought less unbiased than had appeared.

After the trial Robb was relocated in Scotland, allegedly with funds from the RUC. Later he was arrested and convicted on arms charges, and the claim was made that in Ireland he had been a gunrunner for the UVF. Now the issue was whether all along he had perjured himself. Certainly the fact that the victim had been from the UDR, a group not too different from the Black and Tans of a much earlier period, created a reason for local activists to want him dead, and it also created a reason for the RUC to demand a conviction, one way or another.

Rosemary clearly had little liking for the RUC. Lurgan is close to Portadown, where a month earlier there had been first a standoff between police and loyalists and then a spate of rioting in which the mostly Protestant police had gone after Catholic nationalists with seemingly far more enthusiasm than they had shown when they were confronted by their coreligionists. I thumbed through a stack of photographs taken of individuals who had been hurt in the assault. These, she assured me, were a good indication of what justice was like in this area.

Asked if she saw much change coming, she noted simply that the British authorities were cynical when it came to the conflicts between the hard-core Protestant loyalists and the Catholics of the area. I kept picturing Rosemary in a different setting—for instance, Little Rock, Arkansas, thirty years—ago instead of present-day Lurgan in County Armagh. She might have been talking about hard-boiled federal marshals who knew they had to protect the people who were called agitators but themselves had more in common with those who tormented the agitators. I had held the impression that it was mostly young people who caused the trouble in places like Portadown. No, she said, the greatest threat of violence was from middle-aged unionists who went into Catholic neighborhoods. These were the folks with the firebombs. They were also the folks who would not be arrested and prosecuted.

The Apprentice Boys' parade in Derry was now just a day away. Already I was able to talk about our having been among the last tourists to walk above the Bogside along the ancient wall. Later we had watched the coverage on television as British troopers erected the barricades that would prevent anyone from marching the entire way. Talks between Bogside residents and representatives of the Apprentice Boys were at a complete stalemate, and there were the loyalists who said that, just as in Portadown, they would not be denied. The journalists were already assembling, and what worried me was that on both sides there were those who were ready to play to the cameras. I had already decided not to go back up to Derry; instead I would go on to Belfast, where the local Apprentice Boys were being told that they could not march along one of their desired routes that led through the Catholic community off the Lower Ormeau Road.

Lurgan was the first town in which I was made quite aware of being in a Protestant area. There had been an ornate decoration suspended across the main boulevard that proclaimed the loyalist dedication to the Crown, and the streets, like King William Road, announced continued identification with the events of the late seventeenth century. The Catholic area, just by our hotel, had the look of a defiant ghetto with the Tricolor flying from telephone poles and a large poster of Gerry Adams calling for votes. And by the door of one of the private cab companies, most of which were owned by Catholics, there was a flyer calling for information about who might have killed a Catholic cabdriver just a short time before.

I still felt very safe walking the streets, but I was also much more aware of what it was like to be a Catholic in Ulster—not a tourist who would drive away the next day but someone more likely than not to be out of work and dependent on public assistance, living in public housing with the fear renewed every marching season that a mob might burn me out, always aware that I was seen as the intruder who did not belong here. I had no doubt at all that in a place like this, it would only be my natural timidity that kept me from being an IRA man, and I knew also that it might not even matter whether I was a volunteer. My wife, too, could be shot dead in her home, and I would know that her murderers might easily be my neighbors deputized to defend British law. I, too, could be swept up in an internment raid and held for months without trial, offered salvation if I would be the informer and damnation if I dared hold out. I admired Rory, and I admired Rosemary Nelson, and I was also glad that I was only the visitor here, with my convictions never put to the test.

LURGAN: AUGUST 9

It seemed appropriate that the morning began with the banging of the drums as the local contingent of Apprentice Boys paraded toward our hotel in Lurgan. I had just gotten dressed, and my wife was taking her turn in the shower. Quickly I put on the light paper jacket I had once bought as a souvenir at the San Francisco Museum of Modern Art, grabbed my camera, and went out to the street. I had to walk quickly to get ahead of the parade, and I snapped a number of pictures of the marchers and of the RUC who followed them in their armored Rovers. The parade came to an end just a few blocks down, right at the outskirts of the Catholic area. It was early, and I saw very few people on the streets. One young man from the parade came over to me, perhaps wondering whether I should be seen as a troublemaker. Smiling and cheerful, making sure I kept my American accent and did not slip into the brogue that I found myself using when I was around my Irish friends, I got into a conversation about the local Apprentice Boys and was told that there were about three hundred members. I was duly impressed, especially since I was so used to thinking in terms of very small groups when it came to republicans.

This was the first time I had really had a chance to observe a loyalist parade. What was striking was how these men—I noticed no women at all among the marchers—were costumed. Band members themselves had bright uniforms, and those who were otherwise marching in tight ranks wore dark suits with the sashes indicating their lodge membership and the bowler hats that once were standard for British gentlemen. I was beginning to get something more of a feeling for the amount of effort that went into these parades. I could understand how the marching season helped define their identity, and I could even begin to appreciate their anger at any restrictions on their traditional pageantry. For Catholics their parades were "triumphalist" displays calculated to offend. For these men they might be something else indeed.

Several chartered buses had pulled up, and the various marchers and band members got on board for the ride up to Derry. I wished the people well as they left. I did want it to be a peaceful day for all concerned.

I walked back toward my hotel alongside a few friendly RUC officers, who were quite interested to know more about California. I said something about the earthquakes we get, and one of the constables joked that here it was car bombs that caused earth tremors. We parted after a block more, and I wished them a peaceful time also.

I kept walking for a bit more. The RUC station was just a bit down the street, and I was about to take a picture when a car came out and an officer stopped next to me. I asked if it was all right to photograph the station, and I was urged not to. "It makes us look like East Berlin," he said, and he was quite correct. Police stations in the north are the modern-day equivalent of the Norman fortresses scattered throughout the Irish countryside, but they are far less picturesque with their concrete slabs and barbed wire. I mentioned that in the United States our police stations were often attractive public buildings. The officer grunted that new ones were being built that were not as ugly. They were now using a stronger concrete, for instance, so the buildings did not have to look quite as squat, like exaggerated pillboxes from a World War II movie.

I sagaciously refrained from pointing out what was seemingly so obvious—that none of this aesthetic distress would be necessary if the police were seen as the protectors of the entire community, not just the defenders of British rule.

9

The Streets of Belfast

Welcome to Club Noraid, the tour operator that takes you to the heart of the Troubles. Just like Club 18–30 it throws together similar-minded people but instead of offering sand, sea and sex you get Bobby Sands, cemeteries and sanctimony.

Maurice Chittenden and Eamon Lynch
for *The Sunday Times*

BELFAST: AUGUST 10

We were on foot again, as I had returned our rental car at the airport after dropping off my wife at the Holiday Inn, a street over from the splendid Europa Hotel that had been a frequent target of the IRA in years past. Like other European cities built before there were automobiles, it is possible to get around very easily in Belfast by walking, and there were cabs everywhere if it seemed a good idea to save time and energy.

In the afternoon I again walked down Grosvenor Road, over the M1 motorway, past the Great Victoria Hospital, to Falls Road. The Sinn Fein bookstore and advisory center were just another couple of blocks more. This was the last day of an annual street fair held in West Belfast, and one of the venues was the public park across from the hospital. Something was being put on for a crowd of squealing children, and I found myself attempting to reconcile my mental images of the Falls during the violence of the Troubles with what I saw now. I had to remind myself that this normalcy had ruled even then, except perhaps at night, when there were the ritual exchanges of low-level violence between Catholic militants and the British army—gasoline bombs and sporadic sniping from the one and CS gas and sporadic sniping from the other, with fewer injuries on either side than might have occurred at a championship soccer match in Europe or South America when the fans got out of hand.

At the Sinn Fein offices I learned that my friends from Dublin on the Noraid tour were being driven around West Belfast and were due back around four. I took a black taxi—the favored means of travel in the Falls—up to Andersonstown and then walked back to Milltown Cemetery, the final resting grounds for generations of republicans. The first thing to catch my eye was a fairly new grave of a woman named Patricia Ferran, to whom I might have some distant relationship. I walked through the cemetery, occasionally pausing to read an inscription. The city lay stretched out below. It was hard to avoid the thought that there was something highly ironic about this. The eastern area lay like some promised land forbidden to Catholics.

On my way back to the gate, I took a picture of the grave of a man named Alan Lundy. The inscription said that he had been murdered on the first of May in 1993. Back in Los Angeles I would look up his name in Malcolm Sutton's *An Index of Deaths from the Conflict in Ireland, 1969–1993* and learn that he was a Sinn Fein member who had been shot by the paramilitary Ulster Freedom Fighters in Andersonstown while working at the home of one of the councillors. He was thirty-nine, married, and had children. At his grave I said a brief prayer, which I repeated when I looked up his name.

His death, like that of Kathleen O'Hagan on a back road in Tyrone, indicated what sectarian violence was really all about—reciprocal murders in which the victims were often chosen simply on the basis of whether they went to Mass or to services, or whether they preferred the Tricolor or the Union Jack as their flag. These were not men in uniform, paid to risk a bullet to suppress a guerrilla war, or men in ski masks, chancing a hero's death for their cause. One was a political activist, the other a pregnant woman married to an activist. In his book Sutton counts up the strictly sectarian killings—151 by the IRA and the INLA, 713 by various loyalist groups—and omits those in which the victim was targeted because of any more explicit political or paramilitary affiliation. Lundy, someone from Sinn Fein, would not have been counted as a victim of sectarian violence, and Kathleen, who died after Sutton completed his accounts, might not really have counted that way, either. Still, it was hard to avoid the impression that the most tragic killings were not by republican gunmen but by men like those I had seen marching in Lurgan and would see again in Belfast.

Outside the cemetery I found the bus for the Noraid tour. I climbed aboard and began chatting with some of the people I had met in Dublin. Then I stayed with them as they continued their tour with Sinn Fein councillor Tom Hartfield, one of the rising lights in the party, as the guide.

I had been on a bus tour of Belfast months before, but there was a difference between the commercial tour and what was pointed out now. Then the guide had noted the rebuilding of the homes in the Falls and the other Catholic areas of West Belfast. Tom had us note that the new homes were set well back from the street, that the streets themselves were fairly wide and straight, and that the light poles were made of aluminum rather than a heavier metal. All of this, he said, was not for aesthetic reasons. Instead, the urban planning had been centered on the needs of the RUC and the British troops. The wide, straight streets allowed a quick response, the setback homes reduced the opportunities for sniping, and the poles were not very serviceable for barricades.

The murals were a photo op for those on the tour. One near a small parish church led Tom to tell us about the time it was being painted. The newly assigned priest had for some reason or other been offended by the mural and had ordered the people painting it to stop. Ignored, he had called the RUC, who responded by arresting the painters. His congregation then plummeted in membership. This, Tom said, was typical of the relationship between the Church and the republican community. Despite the constant portrayal of Irish conflict as Catholic pitted against Protestant, the Catholic hierarchy had typically sided with the Protestant-dominated forces of law and order. Republicans as a result tended strongly to be unchurched even though their loyalist adversaries trumpeted their own religious affiliations.

Passing by a military base that commanded an imposing view of the city, Tom had another story. Before I had heard how the original flats just across the road had been leveled and new two-story buildings erected that would not obstruct reconnaisance. Tom added that a number of Belfast priests had signed a petition protesting the placement of a new fortress in this neighborhod. All had been transferred away from the area. Only the redoubtable Father Des Wilson remained. He had refused reassignment and had become in effect a worker-priest ministering to local Catholics. I regretted, since his name had come up repeatedly in my interviews, that I probably would not have a chance to meet with him.

I had taken a seat next to a young woman I'll call Alice. In our conversation I explained that my trip was research for a book, and Alice asked what I had written before. I mentioned several books I had done twenty years earlier under my pseudonym of David Farren. Rather hesitantly, I said they had been about the occult, and particularly about the emerging tradition of Wicca. To my surprise, Alice thought she might have read one of them, and she went on to explain that she was very much into Native American spirituality as well as the old pre-Christian traditions of Ireland. She then confided that she was close to a medicine woman who had given her a pouch containing the hair of a white buffalo calf, something that was very much a power object. Alice had in turn passed it on to Martin McGuinness, whom she described as someone very attuned to the spiritual. What she was hoping to do, she said, was to see a stronger spiritual connection between Sinn Fein as a political group and those worldwide who were involved with the earth religions of the present.

I found Alice a delightful companion for the drive, so I tried not to let some of my own cynicism come out. I had heard reports of McGuinness being a devout Catholic, a daily communicant even, and it was a stretch to think of him ever openly expressing a linkage with his pagan roots. It was equally difficult to imagine the New Age types I knew taking seriously the political struggles of this corner of Ireland. Modern-day Druids identified with Stonehenge, not with Belfast and Derry. Of course, it might be just the kind of thing that would delight Ian Paisley, who did have a habit of accusing Catholics of being idolatrous pagans.

At the same time I recalled that in San Francisco the wife of one of the more prominent activists, also asking about my past books, had told me she was herself very much into Wicca and said she would like to have me conduct a ritual handfasting or wedding rite when she and her husband renewed their vows. Well, maybe I would ask around and see if I had been missing something in my previous research. Perhaps even Des Wilson was a covert New Age guru.

On returning from the Falls, I met up with my wife, who had made use of this opportunity to visit some of the stores she remembered in the central city. One problem of going somewhere out of California was that we felt an obligation to pick up a supply of birthday gifts and other remembrances for our four grown children and two grandchildren. Today she had gone shopping for my daughter to get a claddagh bracelet to go with the earrings we had given her a year before. Fortunately this was a small item, since I had already assembled a supply of Guinness shirts and bar towels while we were in Dublin, and we had also made a fateful stop in Waterford to acquire a few additional pieces of crystal.

It was time for dinner, and we walked toward Queen's University and one of the interesting restaurants where we had eaten before. As we got close, we heard the last bangs and bleeps of a parade coming to a close. We went down a side street and found ourselves in front of the Sandy Row Orange Lodge with a group that I assumed had just made the trip back from Derry. By now I felt myself an old hand at chatting up the enemy. Again I took pictures, smiled my best "I am an ignorant but affable American tourist and not really someone out to write about the IRA" smile, and allowed myself to be surrounded by some of the participants.

I asked about the differences among the groups. All week I had heard about the Apprentice Boys, and I knew there were Orangemen, and I had read about Black Preceptors, but just who was who? About a half-dozen men began to explain the differences with a great deal of enthusiasm. I got the impression that it was a rare thing to have a tourist, especially an American, take such an interest in them, and they were eager to have me get it all straight. The Orange Lodges were a religious institution, I was told, and the Black Preceptors were a further group made of Orange Lodge members. The Apprentice Boys were a distinct group. One man, a Black Preceptor, had me look at his watch. The dial had various symbols that reminded me of Masonic imagery, and I mentioned that my father had been a thirty-second-degree Mason. Yes, I was told, there were similarities, but above all the basis for everything here was in the Bible.

"Most people do not know this," one man said, "but the Orange Lodges are an international organization. We have members in Ghana, for instance, and just a few years back we had Mohawk Indians from Canada come over for one of our marches. In fact, you should come inside to see some of the pictures of our members."

My wife and I boldly entered the lodge hall. Someone needed to find a key to the meeting room with the pictures, but soon we were inside and being given the full tour. There was indeed a large picture of the Mohawks in feathered headdress. Repeatedly I was told that the Orange Order saw itself as a religious institution, and it became more obvious that I had been mistaken in seeing the Orangemen as no more than perfervid unionists. There was the Grand Orange Lodge of Ireland, but there were also associated Orange Institutions in England itself and in a number of countries that were completely independent. What seemed to hold them together was a militant Protestantism of a type familiar enough in the United States, especially in the south. Identity was defined in large part by whom they opposed, and they opposed anything connected with the Church of Rome. As one of our guides explained to my wife, using a phrase from early in the century, "Home rule is Rome rule," and it was clear that he really did believe that the Irish government was held in thrall by the Catholic Church.

Two of the men did have the hint of fanaticism about them, the one who talked so anachronistically about "Rome rule" and the other who wanted me to see his Black Preceptor's watch. Fortunately no one was asking about our own religious convictions or lack of them, and I was not especially eager to let them know they were entertaining an ex-Jesuit. I did ask about their perception of the future.

My "Rome rule" man was emphatic on the point that there were a million of his people, and there would be a bloody civil war if ever the Catholics succeeded in getting the British troops to withdraw. This was exaggerated, given that the total population of the north is around a million and a half, with Catholics now approaching parity with Protestants. What I found somewhat disconcerting was his eagerness for the fray.

What about communication between the sides? The first point made was that there could be no discussion with Sinn Fein, since it was a known fact that one had to be from the murderous IRA before he could belong to Sinn Fein. Other efforts at dialogue between Catholics and Protestants were dismissed as a waste of time. True, youngsters from both groups had often enough been brought together, but as they got older, their original loyalties solidified.

I was not sure just what these men looked forward to. Certainly they wanted their own religious freedom, and they regarded any restrictions on their march as preliminary moves in the effort to bring about Catholic domination and limits on that freedom. It was obviously way past the point that they could even imagine regaining control of the entire island. In addition, population shifts, including a higher birth rate for Catholics and increasing emigration for Protestants, meant that soon enough they would be in the minority even in the northern counties. Maintaining the union was said to be as non-negotiable for them as ending it was for dedicated republicans, but it was increasingly difficult to see what benefits there were in remaining a part of the United Kingdom if the northern counties continued to be treated as a troublesome province draining away England's resources.

What was clear enough is that, for good reason or not, they felt their old way of life threatened. Each of the great marches had become a giant pep rally bringing together beleaguered Protestants from everywhere on the island, and the fact that world media were beginning to look at loyalists rather than nationalists as the lawbreakers only intensified their determination to be seen and heard, as though by the sheer numbers of marchers they could muster they would be able to sway public opinion back in their favor.

Apart from the fellow who predicted civil war, these Orangemen did not come across as hatemongers, although maybe I would have had a different impression if we had begun discussing Ian Paisley. They were thoroughly charming gentlemen. One of them even gave my wife an Apprentice Boys pin as a souvenir, and another made sure I had a copy of their newspaper, *Orange Standard*, so that I could read more about them at my leisure. I appreciated their hospitality, and I found myself wondering how different things might have been if these people had ever made the same effort to reach out to the Catholic community as they did to us.

BELFAST: AUGUST 11

It had been twenty-five years since widespread internment was established in Northern Ireland. On Friday *The Irish News*, published in Belfast and regarded as a nationalist paper, had reprinted the front page of its edition for August 10, 1971, together with interviews of those who recalled having been arrested in Belfast on August 9. The original headline had read "PRIEST AMONG 14 DEAD IN NORTH'S BLOODIEST 16 HOURS," and below a photo of a barricade put up in Andersonstown there was another story entitled "300 LIFTED IN DAWN SWOOPS BY ARMY-RUC." Sutton's chronicle of killings during the Troubles lists fifteen who died on the ninth, thirteen by bullets fired by the British army. Soldiers would kill nine more before September, while the IRA was responsible for seven deaths during the entire month of August.

Internment itself was physically and psychologically brutal. Those picked up were often beaten while being transported, then beaten again on their arrival. Torture was routine, with the worst perhaps the experience of being hooded and taken up in a helicopter. The internees were told they were high above the waters of Belfast Lough, and then they were pushed out, screaming. Actually they fell only a few feet to the grass, but they had gone through a psychologically devastating experience. The internments went on until 1974, when they were halted in part because of the worldwide protest over human rights abuses.

Internment had definitely not accomplished its intended purpose, which was to break the IRA by locking up its leaders. Most who were arrested were not IRA men, and most of the actual leaders hid out successfully. Many internees did become IRA men afterward, however, and once again, as had occurred after the Easter Rebellion, British prisons came to be seen as the "universities of republicanism." Understandably, Sinn Fein was not going to let the anniversary go unnoted, and for a dozen years Noraid had scheduled its fact-finding tours to end with the Belfast internment march.

I was up early and walked to a news agent near the Europa to get a Sunday paper. I chose *The Sunday Times* from London and was immediately quite glad that I did. On page 3 there was a feature article about the Noraid tour that I had first met up with in Dublin and then seen again in the Falls. If I had expected an impartial news story, I was quickly disappointed. The artwork that went with the story, a collage of photographs taken of the tour, featured a mock logo of a masked paramilitary with the inscription "Bobby Sands Cemeteries & Sanctimony" and captioned one photo as being taken "At the tomb of the known murderer." A sidebar had a picture of Joe "Godfather" Cahill, identified as having killed a policeman, and proposed a derisive "tour itinerary" that ended "Thurs: Drink in a Provo bar. Afternoon free for shopping."

The article itself, which included a section about Alice and her "miracle pouch" intended for Martin McGuinness, made those who were on the tour appear to be a group of rather dense and easily manipulated Americans. It made for an entertaining read, but it was clearly a hatchet job. What worried me was whether those on the tour might think I was the writer, since I had clearly identified myself as working on a book when I had met with members in Dublin.

In the late morning we walked over to the Falls. Grosvenor Road has a large RUC building on one corner, and lined up across from it were a number of British armored vehicles. None of the troopers seemed interested in checking who we were. I initiated a conversation with a young man by asking the make of the vehicle. He explained these were Saxons, although many people thought that the British were still using the old Saracens. Since I had already started thinking of the RUC buildings as modern-day Norman forts, the choice of a name for these minitanks seemed especially appropriate.

I was curious about the manufacturer, since the RUC armored vehicles were Tangis made by the firm that turned out the Land Rovers favored by American yuppies. To my surprise the soldier jumped down, still holding his automatic rifle, and crawled underneath to see if he could find a name. He didn't, but I told him I appreciated his effort. "These are meant to scare people," he told us. I agreed that I would be quite frightened if I saw one of them bearing down on me. In Derry the past month one man had been crushed to death by a Rover.

Further along, as we got toward Falls Road, we saw the RUC running a check on all vehicles entering the area. Again we walked through unchallenged. I was still not sure just where the march was to begin. A cabdriver suggested we ride on up to Andersonstown, to the strip mall known as the Beehive from the name of a video store. It was next to O'Connell House, the Sinn Fein headquarters. We followed his advice, and my wife had her first trip in a black taxi, the communal transportation that picks up passengers all along the road and drops them off when someone taps a coin on the glass separating the driver from those in the back.

We had something of a wait before the march, which actually was beginning further up, came down to where we were. I took the opportunity to wander around, shamelessly eavesdropping and occasionally striking up a conversation. Then came the marchers, and well to the front was the banner for the Boston chapter of Noraid. I fell in with the group, almost immediately meeting up with Alice. My wife, her camera ready, stayed on the sidewalk to take pictures. There had been some idea that we would walk single-file in three columns, but rebels dislike being that orderly. We straggled and clumped and chatted away the miles down to the Lower Falls and then the city center.

I had picked up an additional copy of the London paper with the article about Noraid, and it was circulating among the American marchers. Alice laughed about it. One of the authors had, like me, sat next to her in the early days of the tour, and she had told him about her pouch with the hair of a white buffalo calf. She had joked that she talked so much, her Sioux friends had given her the name of Alice Longstory. This had appeared in the article as though she had been serious about having an Indian name.

Eventually I spelled someone helping carry the Noraid banner, and my wife and Alice walked ahead of us, chatting about things that I am sure had nothing to do with politics. Every so often, as rumors would come of a loyalist group waiting to intercept us, some of the

Sinn Fein men acting as wardens jogged ahead. There were no incidents, however, although I was a bit surprised when the teenagers in the marching band directly behind us began chanting I-R-A as we crossed over the motorway.

I am not sure how many thousands of us were there in downtown Belfast. The streets, closed off to traffic, were packed solid when Gerry Adams mounted the back of a truck to give a brief speech. There was a skit lampooning the RUC and a little more speechmaking before the event ended. The real RUC watched from a safe distance. They had done their job of keeping away anyone who might have tried to set up a confrontation, although they had made sure that, together with the troopers from the British army, they were ready for anything that could have happened.

I said good-bye to my fellow Americans and thought about the differences between this republican march and the type of parades put on by the various loyalist groups. We definitely were scruffier, and there was an overall sense of this being a community event. Our bands played with enthusiasm but probably not as much professionalism. And we definitely looked like we were having fun, while the men I had seen marching for the Orange Lodge and for the Apprentice Boys were all so very serious.

We did get some television coverage, but it was not that much. No one had thrown a gasoline bomb, and there had been no plastic bullets fired, so the cameramen had little of interest to photograph. As someone on the scene who would have been too tired to run, I was grateful that it had stayed peaceful.

BELFAST: AUGUST 12

This was our last day in Ireland. I started off one time more to the Falls. I kept thinking of how much the main street with its many small stores reminded me of Los Angeles when I had been a child. I found myself nodding much more to people, as though I, too, belonged here. Did people any longer take me for a tourist, I wondered. The strange thing was that I did not feel that much an outsider. For all I knew, I had distant relatives still living in this area, and that should make me a local boy of sorts. Certainly there were many people with my surname, and with more time I would have liked to meet some of them and ask if anyone recollected their grandparents ever talking about cousins gone off to Tennessee.

I made myself somewhat at home in the Sein Fein advisory center. A more organized writer would have set up a series of formal interviews. I had simply drifted into the practice of dropping in on various people and hoping I would find someone to talk with me. At the center a man appointed to intercept individuals like myself kept trying to explain that I could call in advance and make proper arrangements. Then a booming voice from a back room asked me if I wanted some tea and scones. I did indeed, and for the next two hours I talked with a succession of people coming by. What helped, I'm sure, was that I now looked somewhat familiar from having marched along with the Noraid banner.

At this point I did not really expect to get any unexpected information. Instead, I wanted to confirm some impressions I had developed about the men and women of Sinn Fein. One thing I had already noted from my conversations was the degree of humor characterizing the activists. I had met too few unionists to establish a completely reliable base for comparison, but I had made some early judgments. The loyalists were not necessarily dour, but they were earnest and somewhat striking in their seriousness. The republicans were irreverent, no less earnest but almost deceptively light in their expression. I might expect good *craic* (conversation) with them, but I would be preached to by their antagonists.

I am not at all sure whether it makes sense to say there is an innate Celtic style, yet across the centuries I find a certain outlook with the Irish and also with the Scots and the Welsh that sets us apart. I am not sure it can all be explained by upbringing, although I think it is more apparent with those who are relatively poor. We can jest even in the face of death, and we sometimes seem to go out of our way to court our own destruction, as though what matters is to laugh at the one who would strike us down. All right, I exaggerate, but that, too, is Celtic, every bit as much as the old mythology in which our invading gods could be as tall as mountains to wade across the sea.

The people at Sinn Fein found my encounter with the Orangemen of the Sandy Row Lodge interesting. "They would never talk to us," I was told, "so good for you that they let you inside. We never have understood what they are all about." And that, I thought, was part of the tragedy of this situation. I tried to imagine Sinn Fein being a tenth as serious about having the right costumes to march down Falls Road to commemorate important dates in rebel history.

In the afternoon I met up with a man I will call Dermot. I had spent time with his father in Cork, so I already knew that Dermot was himself an author who had chronicled the Troubles in Ballymurphy, one of the Catholic suburbs of Belfast. Although not himself a volunteer, at least as far as I knew, he was sufficiently familiar with the IRA to have a fascinating stock of stories that came out as we worked through a couple of rounds of Guinness.

I mentioned something that I had heard so often outside of Ireland: that the IRA did not represent the Catholic community but held its position solely through intimidation. Dermot was quick to respond. No, during the Troubles the volunteers had most definitely been part of the community. One small indication of this was that people would leave front and back doors unlocked to make it easier for fleeing gunmen.

"There was one house the IRA used for sniping. The owner was usually gone, so they had to break a windowpane on the back door. They would leave a five-pound note to pay for the damages, but finally the owner just left them a key because it was so much trouble to get someone to fix the glass.

"But one time before, there were these three volunteers who are in the house when it is surrounded by a British patrol. They thought the troopers would notice the broken glass and investigate, but they were lucky and the patrol went away. Then they hear a noise as someone is opening the door. One of the men is on the staircase with his rifle, and he has on this Scooby-Doo mask. It turns out it's the owner who's coming in, and he sees the volunteer and lets out a shout. 'Oh God,' he says, 'you really gave me a fright. I thought you were my wife.' "

And then there was the squad that had just got a new automatic rifle. As Dermot told the story, one of the men decided to test it by shooting at the clay top on a chimney. He broke it, but the pieces fell inside and scattered soot all over the carpet. What the men had not known was that the woman living there had a reputation for a fierce temper. She was out of the house with her broom and prepared to do serious bodily harm to whoever had caused the mess on her rug. The volunteers, genuinely alarmed, went running down the street with the woman in pursuit.

All of this was a picture completely at variance with the stock image of the volunteer in films. Even the relatively sympathetic Irish movie *Cal*, in which Helen Mirren plays the lonely Catholic widow of an RUC officer killed by IRA assassins, needed to depict the volunteers as essentially humorless fanatics who could not allow someone useful to them to walk away. In *The Crying Game*, Neil Jordan plays on the same theme of an essentially decent man unable to escape those who demand he share in their murders. In *Blown Away*, Tommy Lee Jones is a psychopathic IRA explosives expert who escapes from prison in the north and travels to the United States to avenge himself on his former protégé, now a police officer on a bomb squad.

As someone coming from Los Angeles, where I knew gunmen might be otherwise personable young kids who believed they could settle disputes only with firepower, I already had good reason to distrust this otherwise consoling image of the accused terrorist as either someone psychologically disturbed or the dupe of such a person. Now that I was in Belfast, either the maniacal volunteers were all in hiding or those who were volunteers simply did not fit the stereotype of psychological misfits. Dermot assured me that IRA men were quite ordinary in all respects but one: they had grown up used to the idea of low-level urban guerrilla warfare. There was no impressment into active service units, for instance. They became fighters as often as not because their fathers and uncles had been volunteers before them, and they were not easily disillusioned when particular operations failed, because setbacks had always been part of the story.

Again I repeated what I had heard so often in England: the IRA was all about drugs and money. Even the punishment beatings and shootings of those accused of drug dealing were explained away as proof that the IRA wanted to monopolize the rackets. Dermot laughed. There were no rich volunteers, and the IRA, at least the Provos, had never slipped into the trap of thinking that revolutionary morality might justify dealing in narcotics. Drugs would destroy a community, and those who wanted the destruction of the Catholic community would be the ones more interested in seeing drugs appear on the scene. To him, this justified the violent episodes in which the Catholic community policed itself.

As I was returning to the hotel, I attempted to see if I could tell who might be a Catholic walking toward me and who a Protestant. I couldn't. This was perhaps one of the advantages the Irish did have over us Americans. The cues might come in a conversation—a difference in accent, perhaps, or the fact that someone's name was more distinctly representative of one group rather than the other—but when mixed together, like the people now on the streets coming home from their jobs or preparing for a night's entertainment, there were not the cues of color or dress that allowed a mob to form like birds pecking at the outsider. The trouble spots, like the Falls or the Shankill, were working-class enclaves where the stranger might well stand out, but they did not represent the full life of this very interesting city.

Was there hope, then? Despite things I had heard and seen that made me wonder—the bigotry I heard expressed in the Sandy Row

Lodge, for instance, and the continuing determination of the IRA to pull off yet another "spectacular" in England, even though this inevitably weakened the credibility of those like Gerry Adams who talked about peace—I began to think it was indeed possible for things to change in the north. I was sorry to leave, because I had never felt such identity with a place as I did now. Yet maybe by returning to California and finishing my book I could help bring this change about.

LOS ANGELES: AUTUMN 1996

I had a small notebook in which I attempted to jot down what happened each day of my journey. Going through it, I prepared the pages you have just read. More happened when I returned home. I joined with my son in playing a greater role as an Irish-American activist by working with a new chapter of Noraid. I met more men from Ireland who had their own stories of life as volunteers. I followed the Irish press by sitting at my computer and using the Internet to call up papers such as the *Irish Times* and the *Irish News* and the *Belfast Telegraph*, as well as republican papers such as *An Phoblacht* and the *Andersonstown News*. I talked to my friend Rory in County Tyrone, and I rejoiced when Colin Duffy was freed from prison and I saw the photograph of Rory and Colin together at a press conference.

Not much more than a year before, I had simply been an American in Dublin, suddenly walking in a march to protest the arrival of the British heir to the throne. Now I knew a great deal more. I had accomplished my first goal of talking with the rebels, in the course of which I may have discovered as much about myself as I had about them. It was one of the perils of being the participant observer, I realized. I was indeed becoming an IRA man, but I still had to work out what that meant.

Part IV

The Past, the Future

One wonders whether monarchy will survive in Britain for many more decades, but it will be a sad thing if abolition of the border must wait upon its demise.

Calton Younger, in his 1979 epilogue to *Ireland's Civil War*

10

How It Could Have Been

They ask in Parliament why we fight on, since clearly we have lost in the field and behave as cowards rather than as gentlemen when we resort to traitorous violence in the streets of London. I reply that we continue our war even in their midst because we shall not be ruled by tyrants. When I recollect the brutal secret executions of Jefferson and Adams and the others who signed our futile declaration of independence, I am not filled with grief or with fear for myself, but with rage and a renewed determination to honor their memories by ensuring that America shall someday be free.

George Washington, writing in Manchester in 1782, fourteen months before his assassination

Of course this is an entirely imaginary text. Washington, with international assistance, did win in the field and went on to become the first president of the United States under the constitution ratified in 1789. John Adams and Thomas Jefferson succeeded him in office. There would still be more fighting between England and her former colonies in the War of 1812, but American independence was never again in question.

It could have ended quite differently. Benjamin Franklin's quip that the Americans should hang together because otherwise they would hang separately could have been a grisly prediction. Imagine that it was someone like General Sir John Maxwell who was in charge of a British army that had succeeded in putting down the American insurrection. It would have seemed urgent that a strong message be sent to other potential rebels, and so all who had signed the Declaration of Independence were found guilty of treason in a furtive court-martial and then hanged in a British stockade.

The British leader had miscalculated, however. The first American revolutionaries, who had engaged in hostilities before making sure they had their countrymen completely behind them, were followed by others who decided to continue the war in a less orthodox manner. By now they did have popular support, and the redcoats were forced to retreat to their forts because no soldier could appear on the streets of Boston or New York without having an unseen enemy shoot at him.

Let's imagine that the horrors of war are brought home to the citizens of London and Manchester and other large English cities when colonial guerrillas, at Washington's directions, engage in acts of sabotage on British soil. Recognizing that this is a war they cannot win, the prime minister and his closest associates appeal for a truce. Washington is prevailed upon to put his signature to a treaty that provides independence to ten of the thirteen colonies, then returns home to head a new government.

The treaty is the best Washington can do. Tory sentiment is very strong in North and South Carolina and in Georgia, and there have been repeated assurances from King George III that these three will continue to be under direct control of the Crown and not under Washington's Free States of America. Former rebels in Massachusetts and Pennsylvania renounce the treaty, however, and a vicious civil war begins. Washington himself is shot dead when he is intercepted by a unit that had formerly been under his command.

For nearly a century more the Free States and the Three Colonies coexist uneasily as an outlaw group labeling itself the Continental Army continues to assert that it alone holds the right to rule the new republic proclaimed by the martyred Adams and Jefferson. There are renewed episodes of guerrilla warfare in England itself as well as in the Three Colonies, which increasingly come to resemble a land occupied by a foreign army. In part the demand of colonials to maintain the tradition of slavery sets a seemingly unbridgeable gap between different groups within the Three Colonies, and the world press records the violent confrontations each summer when slave-owning colonials, with military protection, mount elaborate parades through formerly Tory neighborhoods where the residents insist on flying the Stars and Stripes of the Free States instead of the Union Jack.

This alternative history invites a number of questions. Several deal specifically with the ethics of violence. The first is, simply, What does in fact justify a revolution? Closely related is whether the seeming failure of a revolution removes the moral right of its proponents to continue with a guerrilla war. Assuming that there is such a right, we can then ask, What are the moral limitations of such a war?

The Irish rebels who declared a republic in 1916 were not trained philosophers, but neither were they simply amoral opportunists. The notion of a just war was something they had all learned in their religious upbringing, even though the medieval theologians who had explored the concept only indirectly saw its application in the case of a revolution. The rebels were obviously unaware that to the east a man who called himself Lenin was promoting the idea that conventional moral standards were no more than a device to maintain control by an exploitative class, and so were a function of the supposedly false consciousness for which Karl Marx had reserved the term "ideology." For Pearse and the others, it did seem important to have a justification for their actions that kept within the more familiar parameters of Thomas Aquinas.

Aquinas, in his massive *Summa Theologica*, had set out three conditions for a just war: the authority of the sovereign, a just cause, and the right intention of the belligerents. The Easter rebels, good Catholics that they were, finessed the first condition by insisting that they declare the republic before any shots were fired. As for the theological authority to dissolve their allegiance, there was always the argument of Aquinas that a tyrannical government was not just, and so in this case sedition was not a mortal sin.

The American revolutionaries were not likely to be familiar with Thomas Aquinas, but they did know the thinking of the British philosopher John Locke, whose works dominated the curriculum at Harvard in the mid-eighteenth century. For Locke, a government existed to protect the property of its citizens, and to that end a ruler held his power in what might be called a revocable trust. Just as did Aquinas, Locke relied on Aristotle's distinction between the ruler acting for his own benefit—the characteristic of a tyrant—and the ruler acting for the benefit of his subjects or for "the common good." Misuse of power meant a revocation of the trust through a revolution.

What is particularly striking is how little comparability there really was between American and Irish complaints. The language of the Declaration of Independence, which so strongly echoed Locke's ideas, drastically oversimplified the causes that had led up to hostilities. Instead of a litany of grievances that focused on Parliament's acceptance of the inequitable treatment of colonial businessmen compared with their counterparts in England itself, it is the king himself who is attacked so that the code word "tyranny" can be brought into play.

In Ireland there had been a long and savage history of English abuse that had included periodic efforts at genocide. Only gradually had Catholics regained such elementary privileges of citizenship as the right to vote. There was also an end to the struggle against absentee landlords who had, under the punitive laws in place during the Protestant Ascendancy, accumulated the real estate that formerly belonged to Catholics. From this perspective, the Irish were better off than they had been since the days of Queen Elizabeth, but, in an example of the sociological problem of rising expectations, the obvious disparity that remained became even more of an irritant. Unlike the Americans, the Irish could readily look to London as the seat of a tyrannical government, yet oddly they did not take to using such language.

American citizens, who typically are raised to think of the Declaration of Independence as something morally justified, are seldom as generous to the rebels elsewhere in the world, especially if they seem to hold some distinctly un-American views about religion or politics or economics. In 1916, most Americans were not ready to identify with the Irish cause any more than a few generations later they would identify with the Vietnamese cause or the Cuban cause or the Palestinian cause. The Irish were Catholics at a time when anti-Catholic sentiment remained strong in this country, they had requested help from Germany at a time when we were debating whether to go to war against the Kaiser ourselves, and some of their leaders were militant socialists at a time when socialism seemed a threat to the most basic American notions of the significance of private property.

Americans, fighting for less, did win their independence without the indignity of their first leaders' execution. The Irish, fighting for more, were in large part inspired by such an indignity. Pearse, whose rhetorical reference to "these Fenian dead" in a 1913 funeral oration is a dramatic foreshadowing of his own fate, was made a hero by the British blindly plunging forward to eliminate the evidence of resistance to their rule.

In America, British troopers discovered that their enemy did not require set-piece battles but was adept at fighting from cover. What later would be called the little war—*guerrilla*—when the same tactics were applied in Spain against an imported French ruler turned out to be highly effective. They were applied against the British in South Africa during the Boer War, and Michael Collins made a study of them, adding improvements of his own in this manner he achieved a deadly level of counterintelligence. The enemy no longer had to be wearing a uniform and charging forward with bugle and drum before he was liable to a blast of bullets. It was called murder in England, but Collins saw it simply as war.

Aquinas had not discussed this, unless perhaps an entire ethics of unconventional warfare should be inferred from his pronouncement that ambushes were not morally wrong because they were not "deceptions" in the sense of being broken promises. Michael Collins certainly did feel a concern about justifiying his tactics, although he would not have been that likely to care whether contemporary moral theologians blessed his decisions, but his reasoning did not go much beyond the claim that he had not chosen the field of battle and so had to rely on the weapons available to him.

With the civil war that resulted when men he had formerly commanded refused to accept the treaty, Collins found himself in much the same position that his British adversaries had been in all along. He attempted to escape the fatal charge of tyranny by bringing in the issue of ethnic differences. "We have to learn," he wrote, "that attitudes and actions which were justifiable when directed against an alien administration, holding its position by force, are wholly unjustifiable against a native government which exists only to carry out the people's will, and which can be changed the moment it ceases to do so."

In this statement he dodges the crucial issue of his own government's legitimacy. The fact that it was "native" rather than "alien" was clearly not enough, and even the fact that he might have majority support only underscored the significance of de Valera's claim that "there are rights which a minority may justly uphold, even by arms, against a majority." The central issue was whether the IRA would continue to be seen as the true revolutionary government during the difficult process by which a new country was formed. Collins denied it, just as de Valera would also in time deny it, despite earlier having appealed to the volunteers' resentment.

The English philosopher Thomas Hobbes, who had been close to the exiled Stuarts but wrote in support of Oliver Cromwell, had attempted to base a government's authority on the virtual rather than the actual consent of the governed. As long as the government could keep the peace so that a people did not slip back into a lethal "state of nature," described in his *Leviathan* as "the war of all against all," rational human beings would recognize and agree that they had bartered independent judgment in order to have this peace. Rebellious actions defined one as outside the law, everyone's enemy, unless they in fact proved successful and a new government inherited this virtual consent of the governed. Where Aquinas had not spoken, Hobbes had, and on a Hobbesian basis Michael Collins and his government had not yet succeeded. Accordingly, either the *Oglaigh na hEirann* was entitled, by stretching the point of legitimate succession from the Easter rebels, to see itself as the only continuing rightful government of Ireland or, as yet unvanquished, it had as much a claim as any other armed force.

From 1921 on, this notion has defined whatever can be meant by republicanism in Ireland. Michael Collins was killed on August 26, 1922. The Civil War ended officially on May 24, 1923, with the IRA order to cease fire and dump arms. Nonetheless, in July 1923, IRA leaders did meet in Dublin and establish the organization that has continued to the present. In April a year later the IRA decided to support Sinn Fein as the political voice of republicanism, and Sinn Fein in turn would keep the republican faith by not allowing its members to hold office in any existing government. In September, Clan na Gael, the group of American expatriates who had helped arm the rebels, pledged their continued assistance in order to "secure by force of arms the absolute independence of Ireland." In 1925 the IRA even went sufficiently public to start the newspaper *An Phoblacht*, still the primary vehicle for republican news.

There was continued violence, and there was a continued effort to establish the semblance of a government in exile, albeit in exile within the very country it claimed. Yet there was no progress militarily, and neither was there progress politically. The idea that the cause was futile was simply not allowed into discussion. Instead, the leaders of the IRA compensated for their seeming failure by placing even stronger emphasis on rigid discipline and a clear notion of hierarchical authority. Tim Pat Coogan, whose history of the IRA is an invaluable resource, commented that in this early period of its formation, the IRA was emphatic about the sacrosanctness of its policy, regarding deviations and individual interpretations "with the same severity shown by the Roman Curia to errant theologians."

Writing about the so-called border war between 1956 and 1962, British academic M.L.R. Smith in his *Fighting for Ireland?* comments that the lack of political control—the absence of accountability at the ballot box—imposed insurmountable difficulties on republican strategic thought, so that "it was confined to a few simplistic precepts." Thus its ideology defined the political object (a unified Ireland), the enemy (Britain), and the means to meet the challenge (military action), and yet "it also defined the most likely outcome—isolation and defeat." Hardly sympathetic to the IRA, Smith manages to make a persuasive case that nothing much had changed in the first forty years since the Easter uprising. Unfortunately, there is little reason to think much has changed in the forty years since.

I have asked first about the ethics of a revolution, and now I am asking about the ethics of a guerrilla war following on a failed revolution. On the first count the IRA could claim the authority of either Aquinas or Locke. On the second it is far more difficult to find an acceptable moral basis in the traditional literature, and so I return to my alternative history of the Free States in conflict with the Three Colonies. Exactly what would we say about our imaginary Continental Army invoking the memory of Jefferson and Adams even while it denied the authority of the government established by George Washington? Would we call for a statute of limitations so that wrongs of a particular duration would not any longer be held actionable?

Because the British continue to hold the Tory-dominated Three Colonies, it would seem a betrayal of the first republican ideals to support the Free States' seeming acquiescence in partition. Following Washington's own example, the continentals take their war to London itself, and repeated failure over the decades only stiffens their resolve to bring about a united America. Would we say they were wrong at the very beginning? When there was an unfair treaty? When continued operations only led to more repression?

Let's imagine also that the continentals continue to have widespread popular support in what is seen as British-occupied America. Tories dominate the political and economic life of the Three Colonies, but this is at the expense of the Americans, who are stripped of their property and for a while denied even the right to vote. The Free States, whose constitution refuses to recognize partition, do offer some support for American interests in the Three Colonies, but more often they seem allied with the British against the continentals.

As a present-day American I personally find myself siding with my imaginary continentals. That does not mean I endorse all their actions, and I might regret the lack of accountability of their leaders, but I find their existence justified by the unfinished business of the American Revolution. I want the violence to end, but I cannot accept that acceptance of oppression should be the price for this. I think this analysis of an imaginary situation does carry over to the very real situation in Ireland.

So what of the third issue, the moral limits to the violence of a protracted guerrilla war? At first it might seem paradoxical even to ask the question. After all, is not any war an assault on the respect for life that is the core of most moral systems, and is not a guerrilla war even more an assault in that it completely blurs the distinction between combatants and noncombatants?

Realistically, those who direct a war tend to minimize the notion of moral restraints, and this has certainly been true in the past when England invaded Ireland. The leaders of the IRA, however, have always had several checks on their actions. Even apart from a residual Catholicism with its moral theology of proportional means, there has been the need to base republican claims on an abstraction of legitimacy that runs counter to the notion that only might makes right. It is inconsistent to claim a moral right to rule in the presence of a superior force and simultaneously reject all other moral considerations. In addition, because of any guerrilla army's need to hold the support of the population that shelters it, actions that prove too repugnant are ultimately self-defeating.

Much of my initial interest in the republican movement developed as a result of what I had come to hear about Gerry Adams and Martin McGuinness. These Sinn Fein spokesmen with roots in the conflicts of Belfast and Derry did not appear to be amoral terrorists, ideologues ready to say the end always justified the means. Although neither man would publicly discuss his role in *Oglaigh na hEirann*, each was deeply respected by the volunteers. It did not seem to be a matter of honor among thieves or even the type of regard a mafioso underling might have for a ruthless capo. Adams and McGuinness were seen as good men as well as good leaders, and that meant they were seen as men with a conscience. The question was whether they were clear exceptions, possibly even put forward by their more cynical companions to put a better face on actions determined without the slightest regard for ethical niceties.

Plunging into the literature available on the Irish rebellion and on the paramilitaries who have kept the spirit of that rebellion alive throughout this century, I did find some individuals who might fit the stereotype of the driven and desperate gunman worked over by novelists and screenwriters. They appeared to be exceptions, not the rule. The IRA men of fiction are virtual psychopaths. Most actual IRA men, while not saints, have been decent human beings attempting to limit the carnage of a guerrilla war. They continue to believe that they have never been at the perceived level of their enemy, whether the English mercenaries (with the Black and Tans the most egregious example) who would just as soon kill all the Irish or those comprising loyalist death squads (such as the Shankill Butchers) who would just as soon kill all Catholics.

Obviously there could be extraordinary self-deception in this, as though someone who kills one man in cold blood thinks of himself as morally blameless if another has killed a dozen. Those victimized understandably fail to appreciate the distinction. The critical question was whether any death is justified.

Traditional moral theory has always granted that governments, with a concern for the common good, may act in a manner not allowed to private individuals. It has also allowed greater latitude for actions in wartime. On such a basis the IRA, if it were to be seen as the sole legitimate government on the island, would have little difficulty in claiming to be acting within acceptable moral boundaries. The issue, obviously, is that the IRA is not seen in such a way even by all nationalists, and splits within the IRA complicate matters even for republicans.

It would be futile, I believe, to attempt to defend even the majority of IRA actions, whether these are assassinations or robberies or blowing up buildings or so-called punishment beatings within the nationalist communities. What matters to this analysis is that in the eyes of the volunteer, these are not criminal acts—clear violations of common moral standards—but either justifiable acts of war or reasonable applications of martial law. This was a vision grounded in stories of the 1916 rebellion and the Anglo-Irish War that followed it and reinforced by internment in the British facilities that have been called the "universities of republicanism."

The one thing not allowed the volunteer is to grant authority either to the London or the Dublin government in the definition of his actions. The arrested IRA man's demands to be seen as a prisoner of war—the type of thing that led to the hunger strike led by Bobby Sands in 1981—are not just meant to frustrate his captors. They are essential to his moral self-definition. The only adequate analogy is with the official Catholic view of apostasy, the denial of the faith even under torture.

Violence is morally corrosive when there is a high degree of ambiguity about its legitimacy. The individual does have a number of extreme choices in order to resolve such ambiguity and maintain his emotional balance. First, he can learn to enjoy the violence, and so as the sadist give up any pretense at having a conscience. Second, he can sublimate any residual compassion by becoming the fanatic. Third, he can become the penitent. The fact that most present or former volunteers fit into none of these categories becomes indirect evidence of the success of the republican faith in reducing or eliminating ambiguity.

There are various ways this faith could have been weakened. Had the Catholic Church not officially sided with established forces of law and order, it could very easily have maintained a hold on republicans that sooner or later would have induced a greater spirit of compromise. Had the British government not worked so assiduously to "play the Orange card," the northern counties might have overcome sectarian divisiveness and thus made violence appear so much less a matter of self-defense. The failure of both church and state to facilitate a climate of justice created a vacuum that has allowed the IRA to survive.

I keep coming back to my imaginary continentals. Our actual history has seen Washington and Adams and Jefferson as patriots. In my alternative history they are terrorists. I have not tried to change anything about the men otherwise. If we praise their moral vision and endorse their actions as grounded in this vision, then it cannot just be that we see them as the victors. It is not so far-fetched, then, that Washington might have been compelled to continue his war in the streets of London, or that his former continentals would both reject the authority of the Free States and continue to harass British forces in the Three Colonies. Would their tactics now be morally reprehensible? If so, what has altered the situation in which rebellion was initially justified and wartime actions might seem regrettable but necessary?

11

Playing the Orange Card

For the Loyal Orange Association, as for the many millions of others who feel the same way, the ethical judgment that leads to this conviction of the rightness of the Monarchy is in need of no defence, no justification. The judgment is "a priori," obvious, and certain—that is, it is one of those fundamental truths that need no philosophical base; it is one of the first principles on which all other logical judgments are based.

From an Internet page published by the Grand Orange
Lodge of Ontario East

Americans find it difficult to appreciate just what constitutes the beliefs of those committed to republicanism in the northern counties. It is safe to say they are almost universally unaware of the exact role of the Orangemen and those who define themselves as loyalists. It is obviously too simplistic to say that anti-Catholic bigotry—what is heard in the well-reported rants of Ian Paisley—is the crucial factor, since most Orangemen insist on distinguishing between Catholic themselves and what they see as the evils of the Roman religion. The Orange faith is not just a set of negations any more than is the republican faith, but to understand what it is in positive terms demands a strong effort. I made a beginning in Belfast through the courtesy of the Sandy Row Lodge, and it is through the cooperation of a number of Orangemen and unionists that I am able to put together the picture in this chapter.

The Orange Institution began in the late eighteenth century in County Armagh, and within a century it had gained such prominence that nearly anyone who counted in the senior ranks of unionist politics would be a lodge member. Today there are perhaps forty to fifty thousand Orangemen, a far smaller number than there would have been early in the century when civil war seemed imminent over the issue of Irish home rule. The crucial requirement for membership remains a commitment to Protestantism, and the intertwining of political status and lodge membership effectively guarantees that even those Catholics who are unionists will be excluded from decision-making roles.

In Belfast, at the Sandy Row Lodge, it was a point of pride that there were Orangemen even in Ghana and that Mohawk Indians had marched in a Belfast parade just a few years before. Obviously, this was not something Sinn Fein could claim, and I was made to understand that despite the news stories that only saw Protestant loyalists pitted against Catholic nationalists, the international and multiracial Orange Order transcended the politics of Northern Ireland.

Back home, I kept up some correspondence with representatives of the Orange Institution and was assured that the interests of the various national lodges varied widely. In Canada there would be a discussion of Canadian issues and not Ulster ones. In Ghana, where any political discussion might be less welcome, the lodge functioned more completely as a church. What remained constant was the emphasis on a conservative Protestantism, even though some lodges might be far more secular in their orientation—dedicated to common interests in a craft or trade, for instance—than others. In response to a specific question about what might happen if the British monarch were to be a Catholic, I was told that the primary commitment remained to the Reformed Faith and that oaths to the Crown include the stipulation that the king or queen is in fact a Protestant.

One source for my information on the earlier history of Orangeism is a book that I picked up in an antique shop in Kinsale, County Cork. It is A. T. Q. Stewart's *The Ulster Crisis*, published in 1967. Inside were a few aged clippings and some correspondence on government stationery. One clipping dealt with the effort to return the original ship used to bring illegal weapons to the Ulster Volunteers in 1914, and one letter from the information officer of the Northern Ireland government, written in 1953, included some of the text of the Summary Jurisdiction Bill that restricted what could be published about the preliminary investigation of an indictable offense. Apparently the book's original owner was a London gentleman who closely followed events in Ulster, and I will always be curious about how the book made its way to Michael Collins country. The clipping about the events in 1914 and the increasing limits on public information during the IRA's postwar actions provided convenient points of reference as I prepared this chapter.

Ireland had never been peaceful, but the violence that had closed out the end of the eighteenth century and persisted during the nineteenth was at last leading British political leaders to ask about the wisdom of trying to hold on to this obstreperous province. In 1885, while vacationing on the fjords of Norway, former Prime Minister William Gladstone reached the conclusion that Irish independence was the only solution. The following year, returned to office thanks to the Irish votes brokered by Charles Parnell, he introduced the Home Rule Bill.

Watching from the wings was the politically ambitious Lord Randolph Churchill, who had already written a friend that if Gladstone did introduce such a bill, "the Orange card would be the one to play" in order to force him and his Conservative party out of power. Lord Randolph promptly went to Ulster and vigorously rallied the Protestants, who knew that in an independent Ireland they would be greatly outnumbered and all that would mean for their current status. The bill did fail.

New legislation for home rule was tried again but got nowhere until 1911, when H. H. Asquith and the Liberal party now held power in Parliament thanks to the Irish vote, and a new king, George V, applied pressure to limit the power of the House of Lords. Asquith's opposition came from Dublin-born Edward Carson, who again saw the political advantage in playing the Orange card. Ulster Protestants believed they would not be free to practice their religion in a Catholic Ireland, especially since the Vatican in 1908 had taken a hard line about such personal things as the choice of a mate, insisting that a marriage between a Catholic and a Protestant would be null and void unless solemnized in a Catholic ceremony, itself not allowed unless there was a promise that all children would be raised as Catholics. Unionism and Protestantism were now twinned in Ulster, even though early nationalists such as Wolfe Tone had been Protestants and it was the Catholic hierarchy that repeatedly condemned would-be rebels. The fact that by 1850 Catholics made up a third of the population in Belfast, in part because of the famine driving people from their farms to seek employment in the city, had long ago added a note of bitter sectarian rivalry in the adjacent neighborhoods of the Falls and the Shankill. The Orange parades of midsummer now became annual invitations to violence, even though it is difficult to imagine the working classes of both neighborhoods having much in common with the original supporters of either James II or William III.

In 1912 Carson spearheaded the signing of a solemn covenant to resist home rule. In late September throughout Ulster, and even in the south in Dublin and across the channel in Scotland and England, nearly half a million signatures were affixed to a pledge to resist any effort to establish an Irish government. For a year the Orange lodges had been used as training centers for a new militia, and four months after the signing of the Covenant, these militiamen were linked together as the Ulster Volunteer Force. For ten shillings it was possible to buy a license to own firearms, and the volunteers were able to use rifle clubs as a cover for their marksmanship training.

In September 1913, a provisional government was set up in Ulster, ready to go into action once home rule became law. Everything pointed to civil war, and part of the irony was that senior British officers became heavily involved in what in effect would be mutiny. There were corresponding efforts by the London government to neutralize the Ulster volunteers, but the talk of widespread arrests only intensified Ulster determination. More weapons were needed by the volunteers, and with the connivance of sympathetic officers, twenty thousand German rifles were landed on the Antrim coast and distributed throughout the north. A few months later Irish nationalists followed suit and managed to land weapons for the newly formed Irish volunteers, although in Dublin this led to violence when British soldiers who had attempted to take away these guns were stoned by an angry crowd at Bachelor's Walk by the Liffey. The troopers began shooting, killing three and wounding thirty-eight more.

What kept uniformed British officers from killing each other, as now seemed inevitable, was an event in Sarajevo. A fanatical student managed to assassinate the Austrian archduke, and swiftly a European war was on. Both the Ulster and Irish Volunteers enlisted to fight the Kaiser. Armed resistance to the Crown shifted from Ulster to Dublin and a handful of militants who plotted an uprising at Easter 1916.

Home rule as such had not become a dead issue, especially with the British need to gain American support for their war. Irish-Americans were recognized as having the political power to sway the Congress, and the teaser remained that with the end of the war there would be important concessions to nationalist interests. Amnesty for the 1916 rebels was meant to assuage Irish-Americans, but with the end of the war and the intensifying guerrilla campaign of Michael Collins's Irish Republican Army, there was no longer such a need to placate Catholics. If anything, there was a heaven-sent opportunity to win back the Ulstermen who had been ready to fight against home rule by setting up their own government. Already heavily armed, the Ulster Volunteers were deputized to help British troopers suppress the IRA.

Short of renewed efforts at genocide, the British realized they could not eliminate the IRA, and the leaders of the IRA realized that they were outmanned and outgunned in the north by the Orangemen. Both sides had good reasons for negotiating a treaty that endorsed a partition of the island, even though Collins and his supporters did not see this as something permanent. Tragically, Collins could not hold the allegiance of those who believed they had been fighting for a republic that would include all thirty-two counties, and even after his death and the end of the civil war, events in the north continued to provide the situation that the IRA needed to maintain its reason for existence.

There is considerable irony in the way things turned out in Ireland. The British army could probably never have suppressed a provisional government centered in Belfast in 1914 with the ease that it suppressed a provisional government centered in Dublin in 1916. Had there not been a treaty ending the Anglo-Irish War, most likely there would sooner or later have been a truce between the better-equipped Protestant forces in the north and Catholic forces in the south, and it is anyone's guess whether at that time there would not have been an independent Orange state. Given Sinn Fein's original predilection for a dual monarchy, it might even have happened that it would have been the south that opted for some type of dominion status (what the treaty itself did specify) while the north rejected it.

The main thing to remember is that a certain momentum had been established in Ulster. From the eighteenth century on, Orangeism had come to embody conservative Protestant aspirations. Given their Calvinist origins in Scotland, Ulstermen have always dreamed somewhat of achieving a new Geneva—a true Christian government along the lines of what the so-called religious right would endorse in the United States. As long as the British monarch remained true to the principles of the Reformed Faith, Orangemen would also be unionists, but in their own representative style of organization they were far more "republican" than the Catholics they opposed. In other countries Freemasonry, which had provided the model for the Orange Institution, did demand an end to monarchy, and had it not been for the events of the Anglo-Irish War, Orangemen might similarly have favored a republic of their own.

Ceremonies and trappings, like the lodge halls themselves, allow a visible embodiment of an Orangeman's commitment. A Catholic would even see them as "sacramental"—physical tokens of an invisible grace. What is denied liturgically by the severity of the Reformed Faith, which relies on preaching the Bible in place of the elaborate symbol systems of medieval Christianity, is compensated for with the costumes of marchers and band members in the thousands of parades that provide a good living for all those who make and sell these secular vestments.

Understandably enough, the specific identity of Ulster Protestants has become so bound up with the rites of the summer marches that even slight abrogations of tradition are offensive. Americans, who no longer take religion quite that seriously, have to look to sports to find appropriate analogies. To appreciate the Orange outlook, we might think of the American institution of baseball, which reaches from the World Series down to kids playing T-ball in organized leagues at public parks. Even the fact that baseball uniforms invariably have a nineteenth-century look to them should be a clue to the game's ritual significance in specifying an American institution that has transcended the country of its origins. Imagine, then, that baseball for some reason had systematically excluded Hispanics and so proved increasingly offensive when games were played in cities such as Los Angeles or New York or San Antonio or Miami. Imagine also that the fear of violence led to restrictions on where or when the game would be played. Self-defined "Americans" would be outraged that "foreigners" were trying to drive them out of their own country.

To the Orangemen, the Irish are the aliens, just as Hispanics retain the semblance of aliens in the United States. That the Irish had been dispossessed in the north by Scottish and English farmers and merchants is a historical point of no special relevance, just as in Texas or California it is solely a historical point that these states were once part of the Republic of Mexico. If anything, the fact that the Irish had been dispossessed imposes a Darwinian image of inferiority on them, just as it does on Hispanics in the United States. Losers have no business appealing for justice.

The summertime Orange marches, described by Jarman and Bryan as "a surrogate for low level warfare," provided community entertainment even for Catholic observers prior to the Troubles. For older Orangemen there would be memories of how their fathers or grandfathers drilled in preparation for civil war, and for younger ones out of school for the summer holiday there would be the sheer fun of dressing up and playing an instrument. In more recent years,

as the groups marching have proliferated and the marches themselves have become more frequent, there has been a more determined effort to "take a street" within a Catholic zone, which actually
might have been a Protestant neighborhood at some earlier time.
Opposition only strengthens the Orange resolve, and the old slogan
of "no surrender" comes into play on matters that to anyone else
would seem relatively inconsequential.

This is what I had seen in Derry and Lurgan and Belfast. In Derry
in 1996 the world media had made much of the Apprentice Boys'
demand to march along the walls, yet I was told that until the cease-
fire the route had been closed to everyone to minimize the danger of
sectarian gunmen using the walls to snipe at their enemies. Compli-
cating matters to an extent was the law that from 1951 until 1987
distinguished between "traditional" parades and political marches
or demonstrations, with the marches of the Orange Order, the Black
Institution, the Apprentice Boys of Derry, and other, smaller groups
falling into the first category. To northern Catholics, who did not
engage in religious street processions on the scale found in countries
such as Spain or Italy, this was a distinction that seemed intended to
protect militant Protestants at the expense of their Catholic neighbors. The fact that many constables were themselves Orangemen
only strengthened this impression.

From the Protestant side local Catholics represent a wedge coming from the south. For someone in the north who is not a Catholic,
the display of the Tricolor—the flag of the Republic—creates as
much animosity as the display of the Mexican flag in a middle-class
California neighborhood. This is obviously intensified when it is accompanied by any reference whatsover to the IRA, which succeeded
quite well in disrupting the normal rhythms of life in the north
through its attacks on military and civilian targets. Just as a Catholic
tends to see all Protestants as Orangemen, a Protestant tends to see
all Catholics as republicans and all republicans as IRA men.

As an American in Ireland I found I could move easily enough
from one community to another. Still, among republicans I always
did feel it necessary to identify myself to forestall hostility, but
among loyalists it seemed I could be seen just as a tourist and welcomed without ambivalence. At the same time, when I told republicans that I intended to meet with unionists, there was only
encouragement, but I sensed that unionists in their turn would have
been less well disposed to the thought that I was consorting with
those who seemed so intent on blowing up their cities. One reason
for the difference could be that Catholics were used to having in-

formers in their midst but Protestants were not. As a result, Catholics mistrusted someone with questions but Protestants, such as the Orangemen of the Sandy Row Lodge, were simply eager to make a good impression.

It has been said that there are two distinct and incompatible cultures in the north. This may well be true, but the fault is to think of them in exclusively religious terms, as though marking off Protestants and Catholics in any way establishes the division. Most Catholics are not republicans in any strong sense of the term, and many are not even nationalists. Most republicans come from a Catholic background but are today less likely to take the Church seriously. All Orangemen are both Protestants and unionists, but not all Protestants are either Orangemen or unionists. The best distinction may simply be between those who see themselves as fundamentally Irish and those who identify primarily with either Scotland or England.

That distinction, of course, needs to be considered in the light of the actions of both the British government and the IRA. From the Irish side it is much more than an unequal administration of justice, since the policies in place even before the Troubles were largely predicated on seeing Catholics as actual or potential subversives. From 1969 on, with the IRA harassing the British army and new talk of possibly reuniting the two parts of the island, there was considerable unionist pressure to round up anyone strongly identified with the republican cause. The arrest and internment of 343 Catholics in the early morning hours of August 9, 1971, was a response to this pressure, but it only worsened the situation in the north. As J. Bowyer Bell phrased it in his book *The Irish Troubles*, "The Orange card had been played and burst into flames the hand that had held it."

Once more I'm drawn to comparisons with the American scene. Just a few years before, a number of large American cities had been torn with racial violence in a way much worse than anything that was to happen in the north of Ireland. I remember the situation in Los Angeles in the summer of 1965, the only time before Belfast that I had to walk past armored vehicles and see sentries poised at the end of the street, and I try to imagine what would have been the results if, in reponse to white pressure, all those regarded as black troublemakers had been arrested and sent off to an internment camp where interrogation techniques learned from the North Koreans would be applied to them. There certainly would not have been an upswing in racial harmony.

An entire generation of Catholics in Northern Ireland has grown up during the violence of the Troubles. Those who were young men interned in the British compound at Long Kesh—Gerry Adams, for example—have now become the senior advisers to other young men who wonder how readily they could ever trust the intentions of those they regard collectively as the Brits. If Orangemen see themselves as under siege by Catholic rebels, the Catholics in turn believe themselves targeted for "ethnic cleansing."

Would there have been genuine peace and progress if the IRA, all but defunct after the failed campaigns following the Second World War, had not been revivified in the late 1960s? Again, that is a question that is much like asking whether the situation of African-Americans would have improved spontaneously had there not been "agitators" such as Martin Luther King. It's possible but hardly likely. Catholics were effectively second-class citizens, suffering the worst from unemployment and for all practical purposes excluded from policy-making levels in the government at Stormont that had controlled the fate of the north since the time of the treaty that ended the Anglo-Irish War. A distinct system of criminal justice, set up in 1922 by the Civil Authorities Act and the Constabulary Act and directed squarely at Catholics who might support reunification, meant that civil rights taken for granted anywhere else in the United Kingdom were not to be had in this peculiar province. Nothing had worsened that much because of the IRA, since even the internment of 1971 and the increasing use of state-sanctioned brutality differed only in scale from what had been the lot of Catholics all along.

Could things have been different in 1922? Ambitious politicians had been "playing the Orange card" for nearly forty years from the time Randolph Churchill saw a way to force Gladstone out of power. Edward Carson had promoted the Covenant just a decade earlier. Lloyd George had taken a political risk by ignoring his generals and summoning Irish republicans to the peace table, but neither he nor anyone else in London felt ready to chance the wrath of the powerful Ulster Unionist party, which was to have an official connection with the Orange Institution that went unchallenged from within until 1996. The price of peace with the Irish was a "Free State" of their own. The price of peace with the Orangemen was a type of government that would not have been tolerated anywhere in England itself.

The IRA cease-fire declared in 1994 lasted a year and a half. During that time those furthest to the right on the loyalist side, especially the Democratic Unionist party (DUP) linked with Ian Paisley, were adamant in their refusal ever to negotiate with Sinn Fein. When the Stormont talks first arranged during the cease-fire did begin in late winter, the IRA had resumed its military campaign and Sinn Fein was denied access. An uneasy summer came and went, and there was a collective sigh of relief that the marching season had not erupted into all-out civil war. The IRA continued its actions, in early October attacking the British army in the north with car bombs detonated inside the presumably secure barracks area at Lisburn, outside of Belfast. In response, Prime Minister John Major announced that there was now no chance at all of allowing Gerry Adams and his party to be part of the negotiations on the future of the province. Major, perhaps yet again playing the Orange card, also made it clear that England was not about to relinquish its claim to the six counties.

Is it imaginable that Catholics and Protestants could coexist in the north, actually sharing political power and working collaboratively to improve the region's economy? Bell describes the years before the Troubles as ones in which "each, whatever might be the public position, pursued a life isolated from the other in constant Brownian motion to avoid contact." For half a century there had been coexistence, but certainly there had been no collaboration.

To say things can never change is to ignore the experience of South Africa, in which the system of apartheid involved a far more dramatic repression than anything seen in Ireland, or the story of Israel and the establishment of a separate Palestinian state governed by the former "terrorists" of the PLO. In both these situations, however, the colonial British government had already left the scene. In Ireland it remains very much part of the picture. The north, unlike even Scotland or Wales, is "the province"—an area treated differently, to the advantage of those in the House of Lords who still hold estates there and also to the advantage of the Conservative party that depends on unionist votes to stay in power.

On this basis the Orange attachment to the Crown plays a role in the six counties that clearly differentiates the position of the Orange Institution there from whatever role it takes elsewhere in the world. In Canada or Australia, as in England and Scotland, there can be a delight in the anachronisms of royalty that please the Orangeman and do not particularly offend anyone else. In Africa there can be an even more explicit dedication to the worship patterns of the Reformed Faith, and again it is hard to see why this should prove offensive. In the north the political reality of unionist control through association with the Orange Institution gives the parades a distinct political charge that most definitely will offend Catholics, whether they are nationalists or not.

It may be that the resolution of conflict in Northern Ireland will involve the emergence of a distinct Ulster state that maintains a close relationship with the United Kingdom. Clearly that would be less than what is now demanded by republicans, and to the extent that Catholics and Protestants are treated equally, it will prove undesirable to those who side with Ian Paisley. In itself, though, it does not seem so much a problem that part of a population should identify more strongly with one foreign country than with another, especially if those countries are not hostile to each other.

In my own traveling in the new European Community, I was impressed by the fact that I could move so freely between countries. I definitely began to feel that I was simply a traveler in Europe. In both England and Ireland I watched how students—especially Spaniards and Germans and Scandinavians in England and Italians in Ireland—migrated on holiday from one country to another. In both countries I saw branches of leading American and European firms. If the concept of a common European currency is accepted in the United Kingdom, there would be one thing less to produce the feeling of national separateness in a world that now is moving to a truly global economy.

In Derry and Belfast, I had developed a certain irreverence when it came to the RUC and the British army. I was an American with my passport in my pocket wherever I went, so to some extent I knew I would not be subjected to the indignities that are part of the awareness of any Irish Catholic in the six counties. I had also learned that the Irish, including those Protestants who would resent this designation in the north, are among the most hospitable people in the world, and I really did feel more comfortable anywhere in Ireland, north or south, than I might have felt in an American city. I could sincerely wish the people I spoke with that times would stay peaceful, because I really felt that no one actually wanted the opposite. I did like the Orangemen I met, even though I felt more relaxed with the republicans, and I could understand the inappropriateness of anyone saying that unionists should be "repatriated."

A new, truly secular Ireland is emerging. Whether there is a political border between the twenty-six counties to the south and the six to the north may decline in relevance if present trends continue. The problem really is London, and the key to peace in the north just may be whether there will any longer be a reason to "play the Orange card."

12

The Other Nationalists

Britain created Northern Ireland, Britain is in charge of Northern Ireland, and it cannot now be regarded as a remote and benign referee whose well-intentioned whistle the participants no longer hear in the din of conflict.

John Hume, *A New Ireland*

Liam Neeson, who portrayed Michael Collins in Neil Jordan's film, has commented that when he was growing up in County Antrim, there were still old memories, very quietly rehearsed, of which families had supported Collins and which had supported Eamon de Valera in the civil war. The differences between republicans and other nationalists are rooted in these attitudes of three-quarters of a century back. Those who sided with Collins, and thus supported the treaty ending the Anglo-Irish War, agreed that politics had to replace military action. Those who sided with de Valera, and thus were opposed to the treaty, could not agree that the fighting would be over until the British had left Ireland completely. That is a split that has continued, even after de Valera himself again became the politician and not the warrior.

John Hume of the Socialist Democratic Labor party (SDLP) is the best known of the present-day nationalist politicians. A former seminarian born and raised in the Bogside of Derry and then a teacher, he has been an advocate of nonviolent protest, in sharp contrast to the position of the IRA as well as of Sinn Fein. This is both a tactical and a philosophical difference in approach, and it is explained as much by the fact that, unlike the much younger Gerry Adams, he did not come from a republican family as it is by the fact that, again unlike Adams, he had the advantage of a college education that gave him a chance to live for a prolonged period away from the north. He was briefly held by the British after attempting to mediate a demonstration against the troopers in Derry at the very beginning of the civil rights protests, but he did not go through the indignity of Long Kesh. Instead, with influential legal help, he managed to appeal his fine on the principle that the British Army, sent under an act of Parliament, lacked the authority to arrest him as long as there was a parliament for Northern Ireland at Stormont Castle, just outside of Belfast. He won his case, gaining a certain amount of attention in the process, and the British rectified their legal oversight by abolishing Stormont and having Westminster take over the direct control of the north in 1972.

By all rights, I realize, I ought to be more ready to stand with Hume than with Adams. I, too, spent time in the seminary, and I, too, am a teacher—though I have never had the personal experience of imprisonment. In Northern Ireland, however, my contacts were with the republicans, and somewhere along the way I did become convinced that the ordinary political process was not yet a solution but was itself one of the problems.

To explain this, I need once more to present a history lesson. After the war with Ireland ended in 1922, there was certainly no feeling that any semblance of normalcy would return to the six counties carved out of the island as a lasting British stronghold. One reason was the simple fact that there was a slim Catholic majority in two of those counties—Fermanaugh and Tyrone—and predominantly Catholic areas in every other county except Antrim. Only in the northeast that marked the original Ulster plantation were Protestants overwhelmingly ahead, but this was the center of power in the new province. The political goal was to hold on to the world of the Protestant Ascendancy even in those areas where Protestants were themselves a minority.

The civil war between the original Irish Republican Army and the irregulars spurred on by de Valera's rhetoric spilled over into the north. Even when it ended, there was no reason to think that northern Catholics had ceased to side with the aspirations of the Free State to assume control over the entire island. They could not, then, be treated as complete citizens, and whatever would have been the standards of justice elsewhere in the United Kingdom—or even in the entire British Empire—could not be applied here. The key legislation for maintaining an uneasy control was the 1922 Special Powers Act, which allowed the arrest and indefinite detention of suspected nationalists. In effect, being both Irish and political was now a crime in the English-controlled north, and the accused was by no means presumed innocent until proven guilty.

Tension between the Free State and the north continued. Little that the militantly Catholic de Valera did was about to reassure either England or the Protestants in the north. For example, the Irish Constitution ratified in 1937 contains two provisions, the notorious Articles 2 and 3, that claim the entire island as national territory and uphold the application of Irish laws throughout the north; originally there was another article that gave special prominence to Catholicism. When war broke out, de Valera, while allowing a certain amount of covert assistance to the British, carefully kept Ireland out of the fighting, and IRA men—certainly no friends of de Valera—attempted closer links to Germany just as had the rebels of 1916. Belfast was bombed, and that is remembered to this day when Protestants in the north discuss the Republic.

In the postwar period de Valera's unrelenting prosecution of IRA men, which included an Irish version of the Special Powers Act in the north that allowed arrest and detention without trial, combined with the intense efforts at suppression in the north to bring the IRA itself to the point of admitting defeat. Forty years of fighting seemed to have come to nothing.

The British government has only itself to blame for what happened later. The American civil rights movement inspired new actions among the Catholics of the north, whose complaints of discrimination in housing and employment and political representation reflected the determination of northern Protestants not to surrender anything of their hold on power. Just as in the American south, even nonviolent protests were handled roughly, and now the veterans of the IRA campaigns of the 1940s and 1950s were called upon to mobilize defense against rampaging mobs. The British army, which in 1968 had been sent into the streets of cities such as Belfast and Derry to hold back Protestant mobs, came to be seen as collaborating with the Protestant-dominated RUC in putting down the Catholics. In 1970 the IRA itself split, and the so-called Provos became the dominant faction.

The British government should have seen the importance of a negotiated settlement long before the tragic episode at Derry in 1972 in which troopers gunned down thirteen unarmed demonstrators. As at

Kent State in 1970, where the National Guard fired on protesting students with fatal effect, the failure of military leaders to avoid lethal force marked a turning point on the northern political scene. Combined with the widespread internment of nationalist leaders the previous August, British policy seemed calculated to crush Irish resistance whether violent or peaceful.

In such a setting it took a considerable act of faith to found SDLP in 1970. John Hume, one of the key figures in its organization, had already established himself as someone unafraid of being set upon in a protest, and in this project he had the assistance of other prominent protesters such as Bernadette Devlin. Up until early 1971, according to Tim Pat Coogan's account in *The Troubles*, the army did attempt to negotiate with the republicans in Belfast, but then they resorted to live ammunition. A young Catholic was killed, and a machine-gun-wielding IRA man appeared on the scene and managed to kill the first British soldier to die since the days of the civil war. As the situation became more violent, Hume took his party out of the Stormont parliament in protest. It did not change anything, and Coogan, who as a journalist had traveled with Hume, comments that he simply underestimated the problem of persuading the unionist "that he has to take his foot off the Catholic's neck."

These first years were the worst. Reviewing Malcolm Sutton's *An Index of Deaths from the Conflict in Ireland, 1969–1993*, I note that a UVF bomb killed fifteen Catholics in a Belfast pub on December 4, 1971. On January 30 ("Bloody Sunday") soldiers of the British Army killed fourteen individuals during an internment march in Derry. After that there is the dreadful litany of victims from bomb explosions, often IRA men who died when their own bombs went off prematurely.

The fighting eventually spread beyond the north. On May 17, 1974, twenty-six Irish citizens died as a result of a trio of car bombs set off by loyalists in Dublin, and in Monaghan seven more were killed by still another loyalist car bomb. In November the IRA struck in Birmingham, killing twenty-one people in two pub blasts. And on it went.

In 1973, at a meeting at the cheerfully named Sunningdale in Berkshire, a power-sharing arrangement was signed off that would bring together representatives of the north and the south of Ireland in a common body, the Council of Ireland. Gerry Fitt and John Hume represented SDLP in this attempted coalition. The next year, after a strike by the Ulster Workers' Council, the Sunningdale Agreement collapsed.

In 1981 Sinn Fein, which with true republican intransigence had previously avoided the electoral process, began to contest local elections in the north with its members taking the seats they won. The party also fought for seats in the three centers of power—Stormont, Dublin, and London—but these members, including hunger striker Bobby Sands, would not be seated even if they won. Given the sentiment created by the hunger strike, SDLP had little choice but to follow the same abstentionist policy.

In late 1985, at Hillsborough in County Down, ministers from England and Ireland signed off on the Anglo-Irish Agreement, which gave the Dublin government unprecedented influence in the north. Predictably, the loyalists were furious, but for the first time the members of the RUC, which had few Catholics in its ranks, stood their ground against their coreligionists. The agreement was a godsend for the SDLP in that it provided some evidence that nationalist aspirations could still be advanced by political means. Sinn Fein was coming to recognize the same thing, and in 1986 Adams and the other new leaders of the party, with the explicit blessing of the IRA, ended the abstentionist policy by which republicans from the time of the 1921 treaty had refused to hold office in any government they considered illegitimate. The man Adams had displaced in power, Ruari O'Braidaigh, walked out of the Sinn Fein convention when the vote was taken to end abstentionism and went on to establish a splinter group, Republican Sinn Fein.

In early 1988 Hume and Adams, who now were on parallel tracks in their emphasis on political solutions even though the IRA had begun a deadly new campaign against the British Army in England and in Europe, met and agreed to a series of joint meetings of key figures in both SDLP and Sinn Fein. Three years later Hume began the first draft of a statement he envisioned being made by the British and Irish prime ministers. In August 1993, after several years of secret negotiations, his work culminated in the Downing Street Declaration. A year later the IRA announced a cease-fire, and efforts began to develop a mechanism for involving all groups in a peace process that would end eight decades of violence.

The fact that the cease-fire broke down after eighteen months left both Hume and Adams in a precarious situation. Adams was immediately seen as having lost his usefulness as a stand-in for the IRA's invisible leadership. Hume, who had worked so hard to bring about a political climate in which England officially opened the door to the possibility of independence in the north, now had to deal with those nationalists who had all along claimed that the British were not yet ready to deal with them in good faith.

The exclusion of Sinn Fein from the Stormont talks in March 1996, which became all the more galling to nationalists when some months later the British government mounted a highly visible campaign to reach out and reward loyalist paramilitaries for not breaking their own cease-fire, effectively left Hume as the principal representative of the Catholic side. Given the continuing boycott of Stormont by Ian Paisley and those more extreme unionists who sided with him, it no longer seemed especially important that he was even at the talks. When there was trouble in Derry in July and August because of the Orange Order's and Apprentice Boys' marches, it was not Hume but Sinn Fein's Martin McGuinness who was at center stage in brokering a resolution. In October, when the Apprentice Boys once again decided to march along the walls of Derry to make up for their failure to do so two months earlier, Hume earned the wrath of Bogside residents by openly supporting the march on a civil rights basis.

Hume thus finds himself in the classic dilemma of any liberal. In an effort to be fair, he alienates those who should be his friends while not winning over those who are already his enemies. Himself a decent man with a strong respect for the role of reason in restraining emotion, he urges conciliation when opposing sides are completely unwilling to compromise and see no difficulty in resorting to violence in what they see as their own defense. He is, then, in much the same situation as the Catholic priests who had once been his fellow seminarians: he cannot advocate or even seem to condone violence, yet he lacks the charisma that would allow him to lead traditional adversaries along a new path.

But there is another side to this. I am writing this late in 1996, and rumors circulate about a new IRA cease-fire. Despite the successful infiltration of the British Army's most important base in the north, the capacity of active service units to operate in England seems to have been compromised by a number of arrests. Continued attacks in the six counties are almost certain to provoke loyalist retaliation, and it is not certain that the IRA would manage to hold its own in any resumption of the tit-for-tat killings that came to mark the darkest days of the Troubles. Having had a taste of normalcy, the nationalist communities of the north are not so ready to tolerate the gunmen in their midst. John Hume and his SDLP, all the more acceptable to the British because of a perceived willingness to listen to reason, are thus in a position to be seen as the key spokesmen of nationalism.

What are the alternatives? The people of Northern Ireland—Protestants and Catholics alike—have an extraordinary resilience, and the resumption of violence on the relatively limited scale that has existed since 1969 is not likely to bring either side to make major concessions. Instead, it might only further polarize the two communities, both by further homogenizing neighborhoods along sectarian lines and by further legitimizing the paramilitaries—primarily the IRA on one side and the Ulster Defense Association and UVF on the other—as the agents of their defense. The British security apparatus, including the RUC, would increasingly lose its effectiveness, and while the north would never become another Bosnia or Zaire, there would still be local horrors that would severely set back any chance of economic recovery.

There is the possibility that the British government might prove open to novel approaches to peace. John Major, who has insisted that Sinn Fein no longer has a chance of participating in the peace process after the car bombings at the Belfast army base, might lose to the liberal, Tony Blair, already condemned by the most rabid unionists because of his marriage to a Catholic. The IRA attacks in London and Manchester were against economic targets, and there is some evidence that businessmen in England, watching their insurance rates escalate, see negotiation with the Irish rebels as less reprehensible than bankruptcy. There has already been a proposal from the offices of Elizabeth II that a royal heir might be allowed to marry a Catholic and that the monarch would no longer hold the title of head of the Church of England first claimed by Henry VIII. In such a setting, power-sharing proposals might be much more welcome than they were at the time of the Downing Street Declaration.

In either of these scenarios it is Sinn Fein that is likely to gain support ahead of SDLP. If there is to be a first prime minister of a new Northern Ireland, it might well be Gerry Adams rather than John Hume who would win out.

Most likely, however, is a continuing state of tension that can only benefit Hume. SDLP appeared at the very beginning of the Troubles, has been dominant as the Troubles seemed to be at an end, and still enjoys widespread support. If the IRA does stand down and if the British government persists in its intransigence, Hume's emphasis on compromise becomes more attractive. A central point in his vision, expressed in the Downing Street Declaration, is that the reality of the European Union has completely changed the situation of all the political entities of Europe. If a common currency is accepted to go along with the open borders, there is not much reason for the people of the north to think of choosing between Dublin and London. What would matter most would be the local governmental entities—the traditional counties and the newer districts—and their success in drawing foreign investment as well as in stimulating tourism. The old nationalist–unionist dichotomy would become an anachronism. If this is indeed the future, then John Hume is the individual most likely to move forward as the key player in what happens in the six counties.

13

An Irish Dilemma

Here in Ulster, of course, nothing positive seems remotely possible now—we are all congealed in our little predestined roles, programmed to keep on marching forever to the same tune.
                    Briege Duffaud, *A Wreath Upon the Dead*

I began this book when my son and his friend Kevin Doherty suggested there was a story to tell about the unfinished Irish struggle for independence. At the time I knew little more than what was provided in media converage of the cease-fire. Like most Americans, I had only a dim awareness of the status of the six counties that officially are labeled Northern Ireland. I knew of the IRA just as a terrorist organization, not that different from any other self-styled "liberation army" that has appeared over the last thirty years. Sinn Fein was a political party out to the left someplace. Eamon de Valera was familiar as the long-term president of Eire. I had never heard of Michael Collins.

Over the months, as I began talking with those Irish emigrants who described themselves as republicans, I discovered that there was a deep-rooted acceptance of the legitimacy of IRA violence. Not that anyone in those early meetings would ever describe himself as an IRA man. Even representatives of the groups Noraid and Saoirse, which were concerned with the welfare of those Irish held in British jails, kept the focus on the injustice of the proceedings by which they had been interned, and there was never a clear acknowledgment that at least some of the men and women imprisoned had indeed been involved in the actions for which they were convicted.

Later, as I came to be better known, this reticence faded. With a beer in hand, I watched a film made by a French journalist that showed the IRA in action; with me was a former volunteer who cheered at the footage of a British helicopter being shot down. I looked over the photo album of a woman maybe ten years my senior who had once rented a tank in order to stage a demonstration in front of offices of the British consulate in Los Angeles, and I listened as she explained that growing up in Belfast in 1939, when British troopers would nightly storm into the houses in the Falls, she had wanted to be old enough to be in the IRA herself.

In some ways this paralleled other experiences I had had as a writer. Twenty years before, I had chronicled the appearance of what I labeled "the reconstructed covens"—the Wiccan movement—in several books and articles. The more I wrote, the more I found myself in the company of individuals who not only confirmed what I had first reported but added substantially to it. The same thing was happening now, and I could only hope that my personal history did not repeat itself to the extent that I became as involved as I had before. I did not really want to be an IRA man in anything more than my sympathies. It was all right to talk with the rebels, but I did not want things to go further than that.

Fortunately, the IRA did not think to recruit me. One reason, perhaps, is that as an American I expect too much, and I may be too ready to give up when any particular action fails.

The Irish mood is different. Briege Duffaud, in her marvelous novel *A Wreath Upon the Dead*, attempts to show the continuity of Irish history as the thwarted victories of one generation are remembered by the next. The Wexford rebellion of 1798 inspires the violent actions taken against brutal landlords in the years before the famine, and remembrance of these actions leads to the Fenian uprising later in the century, and that, of course, sets the stage for the Easter Rebellion and then the continued actions of the IRA over the last seventy years. The fact of the matter is that the British are still in Ireland despite all that has happened over the last two hundred years—and the Irish are no more reconciled to it today than they were in the days of Wolfe Tone.

This identification with the past, so unfamiliar to us in the United States, is not true just of the Catholics remembering centuries of oppression. Ulster Protestants, especially those who think in terms of Romanists and papists bent on bloody vengeance, continue to celebrate the memory of the Dutch monarch who came to their rescue against the forces of James II. Whether they are wearing seventeenth-century costumes or simply the bowlers and sashes that link them to the generation of the First World War mobilized by Edward Carson, those who take part in the annual marches of the various lodges and now talk of "the spirit of Drumcree" appear just as determined not to betray their heritage.

On both sides, individuals are insular and insulated in their thinking. Americans, who find themselves in constant migration across their continent and are used to redefining their global enemies and allies, cannot hold on to their past this easily. For us, change is the constant. We grow up with the teaching that we must let go of old prejudices, adapt to new ways, rejoice in our diversity. Even the name "American" bespeaks a break with origins, and in its own ambiguity it invites consistent redefinition. We find an obsession with the past, whether by the Ulster Protestants or the Irish Catholics, something of a mystery. Obviously it hinders our offering advice of the kind that makes any sense to someone actually on the scene.

Not that we don't try. Universally opposed to the IRA, at best marginally sympathetic to Sinn Fein as personified by Gerry Adams, we lament the intransigence of all parties. "If only they would talk to each other," we say, as though it were an absence of colloquy that brought about the Holocaust. The tragedy of human history is not so much that various groups cannot appreciate each other's interests as that so often they can. When in fact interests are irreconcilable, as they certainly seem to be in the six counties, it is the very awareness of these interests that precipitates conflict.

Loyalists do not accept incorporation into any kind of Irish state; Irish nationalists cannot accept the imposition of British rule; the British—hardly honest brokers, as John Hume has commented—continue to play the Orange card for a variety of reasons. This is the awkward triangle of life in Northern Ireland throughout the twentieth century, and there is little Americans seem able to do to change it.

Repeatedly in past chapters I have attempted to draw parallels between the treatment of the Irish by England and the treatment of blacks by whites in the United States. In the American South until very recently, and in the six counties still, there has been rampant discrimination, a denial of access to the political system, and a systematic use of the police and the courts to suppress protest. The American solution was effective desegregation, later coupled with a program of affirmative action. Obviously, drawing on our own experience, we are ready to recommend this as an answer for Ireland.

The difficulty is that there are crucial dissimilarities in the two situations. The most important are that England imposed its rule on the natives of another country, whereas blacks had been imported into America, and that the differences between English and Irish were initially linguistic and religious, whereas blacks and whites almost immediately shared the same language and belonged to the same denominations. Despite the visual distinction between Americans with a European ancestry and Americans of African descent, neither group defines its identity by looking elsewhere. In the north those who see themselves as loyalists see themselves as living in "the province"—an area that remains part of the United Kingdom—and so reject the notion of a specifically Irish identity for themselves. Catholics in the north do claim an ancestral identification with the areas in which they live, but they are constantly reminded that this is today British territory. Integration on the American model becomes impossible because the north lacks the most critical element of such a model: an initial recognition that there is in fact a common culture and a government that in theory can be brought to ignore ethnic distinctions.

One alternative proposed in the north itself, as in the 1993 study *A Citizens' Inquiry: The Opsahl Report on Northern Ireland*, is a model of power-sharing that acknowledges the coexistence of the two groups, nationalists and loyalists. It would favor an Ulster not unlike Lebanon a generation back. This is now the leading example of what has been called an "internal solution," and some idea of how it might work was seen in the 1995 elections for party representation at the ill-fated Stormont peace talks chaired by a prominent American, Senator George Mitchell. Unlike the standard parliamentary system, in which local winners take all and the dominant party effectively controls all political activity, there would be both proportional representation and some system by which group decisions could be negotiated.

This is a model clearly favored by more moderate unionists and by many nationalists. More extreme unionists, such as the group linked with Ian Paisley (the DUP), reject it because it calls for political association with groups such as Sinn Fein. Republicans similarly find it problematic, in part because it requires maintaining a border between north and south and in part because there has not been a sufficient indication of Protestant goodwill. The fact that Sinn Fein was excluded from the Stormont talks upon the breakdown of the

IRA cease-fire has made it even less likely that any purely internal solution would be accepted.

External solutions are those that reach beyond the borders of Northern Ireland. The paradigm of such a solution is the Anglo-Irish Agreement of 1985, in which ministers from both England and the Irish Republic agreed to cooperate in the management of affairs in the six counties. More extreme loyalists view this as little more than a rerun of the home rule debates early in the century that nearly brought about a civil war in Ulster. Republicans also are uncomfortable with it, primarily because it grants the Dublin government an ideologically unacceptable legitimacy.

The one external solution demanded by republicans calls for the withdrawal of British troops, the dissolution of the RUC, and all-Ireland elections to create a new government for the entire island. Clearly, neither Dublin nor Westminster is quite ready for this great an abrogation of their current role, and northern loyalists would almost inevitably initiate armed resistance.

Writing in late 1996, I find it difficult to make any predictions about the future. I assiduously follow the word from the north, and I am told of increased RUC actions against the Catholic communities in Belfast and Derry. This comes after a number of incidents in which loyalist mobs have assaulted Catholics. In one case a mob stoned a bus filled with travelers come for a soccer game, and in another a young child coming out of church was injured by a slab of concrete thrown by another mob. In neither situation did I hear of any RUC action to protect these innocent victims of religious hatred.

I should be used to this as an American, where it is race and not religion that sets the barriers. Blacks, Mexicans and Puerto Ricans, Vietnamese—all have been victims of mob violence when the police have too clearly been on the side of their tormentors. Moreover, I have watched my own city burn twice in vicious incidents of racial rioting, and I once spent an evening cradling a shotgun in fear that white-hating marauders would attack the house where I was staying with my pregnant wife. Why should I be particularly troubled by what happens in a few cities in the north of Ireland when the nightly news alerts me to far more horrifying incidents in the United States?

Perhaps it is simply the fact that what happens in Derry or Belfast or Tyrone or Armagh is more human in its scale. There is the feeling that it all could be avoided if individuals were just a bit more tolerant, as though Catholics and Protestants alike are unable to grasp the message that they are equally God's children. In a large American city the gap between haves and have-nots, whites and nonwhites, seems far less manageable. And so we blame the Irish for their fool-ishness.

What would I recommend? Probably nothing terribly original, though I imagined when I began this book that I would identify an option not yet recognized. The border between north and south does seem increasingly meaningless, and the efforts of the British army and the entire security apparatus of the north to forestall complete independence seem bound to fail. "Brits out" is far too simplistic an answer, given the attitudes of the more rabid loyalists, yet the division established in 1921 has not ever worked.

At some point it seems clear the six counties, long an economic and political liability to Westminster, will be cut loose. Then the crisis will be within the Republic itself, since a unified Ireland might well be a country governed not from Dublin but from Belfast. Loyalists, who originally were ready to bolt from the security of the United Kingdom when something far less than full independence was under discussion for the Irish, might then indeed fight to establish an en-clave of their own, and that would be still another crisis. The cliché "out of the frying pan, into the fire" might apply all too well, and Ireland might then seem even further away from the goal of a single, united country.

My own conviction after more than a year of reading and talking and traveling is that the IRA itself is not the problem, but it remains to be seen whether it can actually be part of the solution. The British government does hold the key to any peaceful resolution, yet, with the Orange card still being played for political advantage, London's intransigence has only made the situation worse than it was when the last cease-fire was arranged. Clearly, the IRA cannot win militar-ily against the full force of the British army, but it is just as vital to note that neither can it be defeated.

Suggestions for Further Reading

There is now a considerable library of good works on the Irish situation, past and present. I cannot list them all, but I will mention some that I have found particularly useful in my own research. Many others still sit on my shelves, unread in the crush of other business.

On the general history of Ireland there is R. F. Foster's *Modern Ireland 1600–1972* (Allen Lane, Penguin Press, 1988). For the north there is Jonathan Bardon's *A History of Ulster* (Blackstaff Press, 1992).

The Easter Uprising is covered dramatically in Peter de Rosa's *Rebels: The Irish Uprising of 1916* (Fawcett Columbine, 1990) and in Max Caulfield's *The Easter Rebellion* (Roberts Rinehart, 1995). Key figures are presented in two wonderful biographies by Tim Pat Coogan—*Michael Collins: The Man Who Made Ireland* (Roberts Rinehart, 1996) and *Eamon de Valera: The Man Who Was Ireland* (Harper Perennial, 1996).

The period since 1966 is covered in a number of books, most notably Tim Pat Coogan's *The Troubles: Ireland's Ordeal 1966–1996 and the Search for Peace* (Roberts Rinehart, 1996) and J. Bowyer Bell's *The Irish Troubles: A Generation of Violence, 1967–1992* (St. Martin's Press, 1993). The IRA, past and present, is discussed by Tim Pat Coogan in *The IRA: A History* (Roberts Rinehart, 1994) and J. Bowyer Bell in *The Gun in Politics: An Analysis of Irish Political Conflict, 1916–1986* (Transaction, 1991). I would also recommend a very personal book by Kevin Toolis, *Rebel Hearts: Journeys Within the IRA's Soul* (Picador,

1995). A look at his life by someone who had been on active services is Shane O'Doherty's *The Volunteer: A Former IRA Man's True Story* (Fount, 1993).

Journalists who have tried to track the ins and outs of the often violent transitions within the ranks of those who have picked up the gun include Patrick Bishop and Eamonn Mallie, *The Provisional IRA* (Corgi, 1994), and Jack Holland and Henry McDonald, *INLA: Deadly Divisions* (Torc, 1994). Striking books by former republican prisoners are Gerry Adams's *Cage Eleven* (Brandon, 1990) and *Nor Meekly Serve My Time: The H Block Struggle 1976–1981*, compiled by Brian Campbell (Beyond the Pale, 1994). Padraig O'Malley discusses the hunger strike of 1981 in *Biting at the Grave: The Irish Hunger Strikers and the Politics of Despair* (Beacon, 1990), and there is also David Beresford's *Ten Men Dead* (HarperCollins, 1994).

Life in the north during the Troubles is chronicled by Tony Parker in *May the Lord in His Mercy Be Kind to Belfast* (Henry Holt, 1994), by John Conroy in *Belfast Diary: War as a Way of Life* (Beacon, 1995), and by Eamonn McCann in *War and an Irish Town* (Pluto, 1993).

Other books of interest are Brendan O'Brian's *The Long War: The IRA and Sinn Fein 1985 to Today* (Syracuse University Press, 1995) and Padraig O'Malley's *The Uncivil Wars: Ireland Today* (Beacon, 1990).

Finally, there are two stunning novels—Eoin McNamee's *Resurrection Man* (Picador USA, 1994), based on the deadly career of Lenny Murphy and the Shankill Butchers, and Briege Duffaud's *A Wreath Upon the Dead* (Poolbeg, 1993).

Index

About the Author

DOUGLASS McFERRAN was trained to be a Jesuit priest but withdrew from the order after ten years. Since 1966 he has been teaching philosophy at Los Angeles Pierce College. He has written several books and a number of articles on the contemporary witchcraft movement.